OPEN SECRETS OF THE ANTICHRIST

Has the beast of Bible prophecy identified itself?

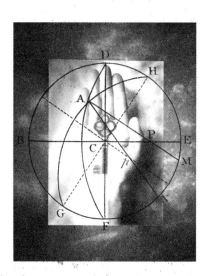

Donald Ernest Mansell

Pacific Press® Publishing Association

Nampa, Idaho
Oshawa, Ontario, Canada
www.pacificpress.com

Edited by David C. Jarnes
Designed by Dennis Ferree
Cover art by Allen Wallace/PHOTONICA

Copyright © 2002 by
Pacific Press® Publishing Association
Printed in the United States of America
All Rights Reserved

Additional copies of this book may be purchased at
http://www.adventistbookcenter.com

Library of Congress Cataloging-in-Publication Data:

Mansell, Donald Ernest, 1923-
    Open secrets of the Antichrist : has the beast of prophecy identi-
fied itself? / Donald Ernest Mansell.
    p. cm.
    Includes bibliographical references.
    ISBN 0-8163-1862-X (pbk.)
    1. Antichrist. 2. Bible. O.T. Daniel—Prophecies. I. Title

BS1556 .M28 2002
236—dc21   2001036646

02 03 04 05 06 • 5 4 3 2 1

Contents

Dedicated to the memory of our parents,
Ernest P. and Edith W. Mansell and
Fay S. and Emily S. West

Preface

Some of the finest, most dedicated and self-sacrificing Christians in the world are Roman Catholics—Mother Teresa, who devoted a lifetime in ministry to the untouchables of India; Father Damien, who requested that he be sent to the leper colony in Molokai, Hawaii, where he labored until his death from leprosy; and Father Kolbe, who, in a Nazi concentration camp, volunteered to die in place of Sgt. Franciszek Gajowniczek, to name but a few. The vast majority of the communicants of this church are unaware that the papal hierarchy, apparently unwittingly, identifies itself as being the Antichrist of Bible prophecy. Because the evidence for this conclusion is so compelling, it may appear to some readers that the objective of this book is to bash Catholics. That is not its intent. Its primary purpose is to enlighten Christians of all faiths that from the papal hierarchy's own statements, claims, and interpretations, corroborated by non-Catholic authorities, the papal system is, regrettably, the prophesied Antichrist.

Catholic scholars identify the "woman" of Revelation 12 as symbolic of a church—their church. In Revelation 17 a "woman," called "Babylon," who sits on "seven hills," is identified by many of these same scholars as being "Rome." If the woman of Revelation 12 symbolizes a church, then, by the same token, the woman of Revelation 17 also symbolizes a church. This leads to the secondary purpose of this book. In

Revelation 18, "a voice . . . from heaven" exhorts God's "people" who are in "Babylon" to "come out . . . from her" (The New Jerusalem Bible [a Catholic Bible]). Jesus says in John 10:16 that He has a fold—a church. Then He adds, " 'Other sheep I have which are not of this fold; them also I must bring, and they shall hear my voice; and there shall be one fold, and one shepherd.' " We believe that the voice from heaven calling God's people out of Babylon is the voice of Jesus calling His sheep into His fold. It is the hope and fervent prayer of this author that many in the Babylonian—and other folds—will respond to heaven's urgent exhortation and join the "remnant" of Revelation 12:17, who "keep the commandments of God and have the testimony of Jesus Christ."

. . . . .

In the preparation of this book I have been deeply indebted to Vesta, my wife and best friend of fifty years. Without her help and encouragement this book would never have been written. However, any errors or mistakes found herein are not hers, or anyone else's. They are entirely my own.

Donald Ernest Mansell

CHAPTER ONE

The Prophecy of Daniel Seven

Pope John Paul II was addressing the European Parliament in Strasbourg, France, on October 11, 1988, when the Rev. Ian Paisley* suddenly leaped to his feet and, pointing an accusing finger at the Pontiff, yelled, "I denounce† you as the Antichrist!"[1] Paisley was quickly silenced as security guards moved in and unceremoniously ushered him out of the chamber.

Regardless of one's religious beliefs, most everyone will agree that such behavior is rude and reprehensible. One seldom sees such unseemly deportment these days, but in centuries past it was not uncommon for both Protestants and Roman Catholics to hurl epithets at one another. For example, for three hundred years following the Reformation, Protestants accused the Roman Catholic hierarchy headed by the pope (usually called the papacy[2]) of being the "little horn" of Daniel 7 and branded it the Antichrist. Interestingly, a footnote on Daniel 7:8 in the Roman

---

* The Rev. Ian Paisley is a Fundamentalist preacher and a representative of the Democratic Union Party of North Ireland.

† The Religious News Service reported that Paisley said, "I renounce you . . . " It seems far more likely that he said, or at least meant to say, "I denounce you . . ."

Catholic-approved Douay-Rheims Version says concerning this horn: *"Another little horn. This is commonly understood of Antichrist."*[3]

"Antichrist" is a combination of two Greek words, *ante,* which, unlike our prefix "anti," means both "against" and "in place of" and *Christos,* "Christ." In other words, Antichrist is a religious system that, professing to take the place of Christ, in reality opposes Him in doing so.[*]

To label a person or a religious system Antichrist is to level an odious charge. Fairness demands that we take seriously the testimony of the accused rather than the slanderous imputations of individuals like Paisley or the attributions of the Catholic-hating Protestants of Reformation times.

In Daniel 7, this prophet saw four beasts rise out of the sea. The fourth beast had ten horns, three of which were displaced by a "little horn," which becomes the focus of attention because it blasphemes God and persecutes His people. The vision ends with judgment rendered in favor of God's people and executed against the little horn. (For the reader's convenience, the appendix to this book contains the whole of Daniel 7, quoted from the Roman Catholic New American Bible [NAB].)

While Daniel was deeply concerned with the "fourth beast" and its "ten horns," he was far more distressed by the "little horn" and its activity against the holy ones of the Most High (see Dan. 7:8, 19-21). Hence, while this chapter will identify the fourth beast and the ten horns, it will focus especially on the little horn. Subsequent chapters will examine in depth the identity and duration of the little horn, the relation of Daniel 8 and 12 to chapter 7, and the events foretold to take place in "the time of the end."

What the four beasts represent

The four animals in this prophecy are plainly declared to "stand for four kingdoms which shall arise on the earth" (v.17). So the ques-

---

[*] See Cardinal Newman's description of Antichrist in the second paragraph of his defense of his church, quoted on page 24 of this book.

tion is: What kingdoms do these creatures represent? A footnote in the Douay-Rheims Version gives the following interpretation: "Chap. 7. Ver. 3. *Four great beasts.* The Chaldean, Persian, Grecian and Roman empires."[4]

Although the footnote goes on to give another explanation, Catholics and the Protestant Reformers were on common ground with respect to this interpretation of the four symbolic beasts of Daniel 7. Consequently, this common ground will be taken as the starting point of this study.

Virtually every history book on western civilization confirms the above sequence of empires. Beginning with the time the vision was given (553/552 B.C.), the Chaldean, also known as the Babylonian Empire, was followed by the Persian, otherwise known as the Medo-Persian Empire, then the Grecian, also called the Macedonian Empire, and lastly the Roman Empire.

Daniel 7:24 says, "The ten horns . . . [are] ten kings rising out of" the fourth kingdom, which according to the Douay-Rheims Version, was the Roman Empire. It follows, therefore that the "little horn" that "sprang out of the midst of these horns" (v. 8) must also be a king and that he too would rise out of the Roman Empire.

Daniel 7 further says that the little-horn king would "rise up after" the ten kings appeared (v. 24); that as he "sprang up," "three of the previous" horns or kings would be "torn away" or laid "low" "to make room for" him (vs. 8, 24, 8); and that although a king, he would be "different from his fellows." The difference would be that he would have "eyes like a man" and "a mouth that . . . [would speak] arrogantly" "against the Most High" (vs. 24, 20, 8, 25).

It also says that this little-horn king would become "greater than . . . [his] fellows" (v. 20); that he would "oppress the holy ones of the Most High" (v. 25); that he would think "to change the feast days and the law" (v. 25); and that he would have power to persecute the holy ones of the Most High "for a year, two years, and a half-year" (v. 25).

What the ten horns represent

If the fourth beast is the Roman Empire, as the Protestant Reformers and the footnote in the Douay-Rheims Version both claimed, who are the "ten kings" that were to arise "before" the Antichrist, the "different" little-horn king, "sprang up" (vs. 24, 20)? A footnote on Daniel 7:7 in the Douay-Rheims Version gives this interpretation: "Ver. 7. *Ten horns.* That is, ten kingdoms, (as Apoc. 17, 12 [i.e., Rev. 17:12]) among which the empire of the fourth beast [Rome] shall be parceled."

Was the Roman Empire parceled out among some ten kingdoms when it broke up? The Douay-Rheims Version footnote on this verse acknowledges that it was, and the Protestant Reformers said the same.

Father Joseph Turmel, a French Roman Catholic priest and theologian, confirms what the Douay-Rheims Version footnote says. Writing under the pseudonym of André Lagarde, he describes the breakup of the Western Roman Empire. Says he:

> The Empire was falling into decay. The Barbarians knew that its life was failing, that the old organism was worn out, and they hastened to take possession of the remains. From every direction they came for the spoils. The Saxons and the Angles settled in Great Britain; the Franks invaded Northern Gaul; the Visigoths made Spain and the reigion south of the Loire their own; the Burgundians took possession of the upper valley of the Rhone; the Vandals made conquests in Africa. The Ostrogoths and Lombards were waiting for their turn to come. Among these new invaders some were heretics, others were pagans.

When Turmel says that some of the barbarians were heretics, he means that they were Arians. Unlike most Catholic Christians within the Roman Empire, the majority of the barbarian tribes that parceled out that empire were followers of Arius, presbyter of Alexandria (d. A.D. 336), who denied that "the man Christ Jesus" (1 Tim. 2:5) was of the same essence as the Father. It is for this reason that Turmel calls the barbarian tribes that rejected the doctrine of the full deity of Christ "heretics."

The article "Arianism" in the *New Catholic Encyclopedia* (1967 ed.), says that

> the Germanic Christians were known as Arians. Despite some persecution, Christianity in this form spread with remarkable vigor from the Goths to the neighboring tribes, such as the Gepides, Herules, Vandals, Suevi, Alamanni, and Burgundians. When they invaded the West[ern Roman Empire] and established the various Germanic kingdoms, most of these tribes professed homoeism [another term for Arianism] as their national religion and in some instances persecuted those among the Roman population who professed Catholic orthodoxy.
>
> This religious division, added to the ethnic antagonism, retarded the unification of the Roman and barbarian peoples; but gradually the Catholic Church succeeded in eliminating Arianism. In some instances this was achieved by military action that all but wiped out the Germanic element: in 553* the Vandals in Africa were utterly destroyed by the armies of Justinian I; and in 552 the Ostrogothic kingdom of Italy suffered a similar fate.[6]

The Ostrogoths exterminated the Herules, or Heruls, briefly mentioned in this source, in 493.

C. Mervyn Maxwell, late professor of church history at Andrews University, confirms the above explanation of what happened in the breakup of the Roman Empire and adds some interesting corroborating details. He says:

---

* The *Encyclopedia's* article "Vandals" correctly gives the date as 534, rather than 553.

Zeno, the Eastern Roman Emperor (474-491), grew increasingly fearful of the Arian Ostrogoths, who were encamped in a reserve not far from Constantinople, where they were becoming increasingly restless. At the same time Zeno was deeply concerned about the Arian Heruls in Italy, whose leader, Odovacar, in 476 had removed the last of the Western Roman Emperors and had proclaimed himself king. (This action of Odovacar's is viewed as marking the "fall of the [Western] Roman Empire.")

In 487 Zeno officially commissioned Theodoric, leader of the Ostrogoths, to march to Italy and dispose of the Heruls. . . . [A]fter five years of fighting, the Ostrogoths . . . destroyed the Heruls, who disappeared from history. Thus the Catholic emperor Zeno accomplished the elimination of one of the Arian horns. . . .

In the 530s Justinian [emperor of the Eastern Roman Empire from 526 to 565] launched a holy war against the Arian Vandals and the Arian Ostrogoths. . . .

Justinian commissioned his finest general, Belisarius, to sail with an army from Constantinople to North Africa and destroy the Vandals. After the crucial battle of Tricamarum, the Vandals in 534 "disappeared like a mist," says the *Shorter Cambridge Medieval History.*

Belisarius, obeying orders, then turned north against the Arian Ostrogoths in Italy. . . . In December 536 he marched unopposed into Rome with a mere 5,000 men. The Ostrogoths counterattacked by surrounding Rome with 150,000 men (Procopius says), making Belisarius a prisoner inside the city he hoped to liberate. . . .

The Goths then foolishly cut the fourteen aqueducts leading into Rome in the hope of driving Belisarius to surrender from lack of water. But the torrents that poured from the broken aqueducts created a quagmire that bred malarial mosquitoes and caused epidemics. The large Gothic army was so grievously reduced by disease that in March 538 Belisarius with his small force was able to defeat it handily.[7]

Although the Ostrogoths were not completely destroyed until 553, their defeat by Belisarius in 538 laid "low" (Catholic Study Bible), or, as Maxwell says, "significantly broke the power of," the Arian Ostrogoths.[8] Henceforth, the bishop of Rome was free to rise to a position of dominance in western Europe, as the *New Catholic Encyclopedia* clearly implies.

The "different" little-horn king

A kingdom is ruled by a succession of rulers—in other words, a dynasty or dynasties—not by a single monarch. Hence, the barbarian kingdoms, among which the Western Roman Empire was parceled, were each ruled by successions of kings. It follows, therefore, that the little horn represents a kingdom with its succession of rulers, *not a kingdom with only one king* (see *The Catholic Encyclopedia's* definition of *papacy* in this chapter's endnote 2). *The interpretation that in the prophecies of Daniel and the Revelation a horn symbolizes a kingdom with its succession of kings is of critical importance to this study and cannot be emphasized too strongly.*

Specifically in reference to the Roman Catholic Church, Malachi Martin—a former Jesuit professor at the Vatican's Pontifical Biblical Institute and the author of the bestseller *The Keys of This Blood*, agrees with this definition. He says that the

> churchly organization is aptly described as a "kingdom," or "monarchy," with all the classical connotations of those terms: a hierarchical structural pattern; a single authoritative head—the Pope—delegating authority throughout the structure.[9]

Note, however, that in this prophecy, the little horn was declared to be "different" from the other horns (v. 24). It is not surprising, therefore, that, *unlike* the horns that preceded it, the "little horn" had a "mouth that spoke arrogantly" "against the Most High," it oppressed "the holy ones of the Most High," and it attempted to change "the feast days and the law" (vs. 8, 25). These activities clearly have religious implications. Therefore, besides being a succession of political kings, the little horn was also a religious kingdom, or, to put it another way, the little horn was to be a *religio-political dynasty.*

As previously pointed out, the Douay-Rheims Version identifies this religio-political dynasty with Antichrist. In other words, Antichrist was to be a religio-political succession of rulers, yet ruled at any given time by a single ruler.

In light of the characteristics specified by Daniel 7 and substantiated by Roman Catholic (as well as Protestant) interpretations, can the Protestant Reformers be faulted for identifying the little horn with the papacy? To ask the question is to answer it; what other conclusion could the Reformers come to than that the papacy, *by its own terms,* was Antichrist?

But, as will now be shown, the astonishing thing is that Roman Catholics themselves have openly called the pope or the papal succession "Antichrist"!

As early as A.D. 991, more than five hundred years before there was a Protestant, Arnulf, Bishop of Orleans, France, accused the Roman pontiff of being "Antichrist, sitting in the temple of God, and demeaning himself as a god."[10]

Again, in 1240, centuries before Protestantism arose, Eberhard II, Archbishop of Salzburg, Austria, wrote that the people of his day—in other words, Roman Catholics—were "accustomed" to calling the pope "Antichrist." Eberhard himself, obliquely, but unmistakably, pointed to the papal system as the little horn of Daniel 7. He said:

> Ten kings exist at the same time, who have divided the circle of the earth, formerly the Roman empire, not for ruling but for destroying. There are ten horns, that which seemed incredible to divine Aurelius Augustine; the Turks, the Greeks, the Egyp-

tians, the Africans, the Spaniards, the Gauls, the English, the Germans, the Sicilians, the Italians possess the Roman provinces and have cut off the Roman colonists in these parts. And a little horn has sprung up under these, which has eyes and a mouth speaking great things; he reduces to order the three most powerful kingdoms of Sicily, Italy, and Germany, and compels them to serve him; with an unendurable lordship he plagues the people of Christ, and the saints of God; he mingles divine and human things, he sets in motion the abominable and the detestable things. What is more clear than this prophecy? All the signs and wonders which that heavenly teacher of ours pointed out to us (unroll the chronicles) have been fulfilled long ago.[11]

While the Reformers might not have agreed with every detail of Eberhard's interpretation, the vital point is that here are Roman Catholic prelates, and even the Roman Catholic laity, calling the pope or the papal system "Antichrist."

Since this is such a serious charge, no one should conclude that the papal system is Antichrist without indisputable supporting testimony. Therefore in the next chapter we will present statements from Roman Catholic sources and compare them with the specifications of Daniel's prophecy.

---

1. *Religious News Service,* "Fundamentalist yells, nude statues fail to deter the Pope." Release dated 10-12-88, no. 8954. Additional facts gleaned from statements made by those who saw the telecast.

2. *The Catholic Encyclopedia* (New York: Robert Appleton Company, 1911), art. "Papacy," vol. 11, p. 451. *Imprimatur:* John M. Farley, Archbishop of New York: "Papacy. The ecclesiastical system in which the pope as successor of St. Peter and Vicar of Jesus Christ governs the Catholic Church as its supreme head."

3. *The Holy Bible: The Catholic Bible: Douay-Rheims Version* (San Francisco: Benziger Brothers, Inc., 1941). Footnote on Dan. 3. *Nihil Obstat:* Arthur J. Scanlan, S.T.D., *Censor*

Librorum. Imprimatur: Francis J. Spellman, D.D., Archbishop of New York. New York, February 3, 1941. Abbreviated *D-R.*

4. *D-R:* Dan. 7:3, footnote.

5. André Lagarde [pseudonym for Fr. Joseph Turmel], *The Latin Church in the Middle Ages* (New York: Scribner, 1915), v, vi. Quoted in *Bible Students' Source Book,* Don F. Neufeld, Julia Neuffer, eds. (Washington, D.C.: Review and Herald Publishing Association, 1962), 690.

6. *New Catholic Encyclopedia* (San Francisco: McGraw-Hill Book Company, 1967), art., "Arianism," vol. 1, p. 794. *Nihil Obstat:* John P. Whalen, M.A., S.T.D., Censor Deputatis. *Imprimatur:* Patrick A. O'Boyle, D.D., Archbishop of Washington, August 5, 1966.

7. C. Mervyn Maxwell, *God Cares* (Nampa, Idaho: Pacific Press Publishing Association, 1981), 145, 146.

8. Ibid., 129.

9. Malachi Martin, *The Keys of This Blood* (New York: Simon & Schuster, 1990), 604.

10. Abel Francois Villemain, *The Life of Gregory the Seventh,* James Baber Brockley, trans. (London: Richard Bentley and Son, 1874), 1:175, 176. Quoted by LeRoy Edwin Froom in *The Prophetic Faith of Our Fathers* (Hagerstown, Md.: Review and Herald Publishing Association, 1950), 1:542. (Abbreviated *Prophetic Faith,* vol. 1, vol. 2, etc.)

11. Johannes Turmair, pseudonym Ioannes Aventino, *Annalium Boiorum Libri Septem* (Ingoldstadt: Per Alexandrum & Samuelem Weissenhorn, 1554), 685. Quoted in *Prophetic Faith,* 1:801.

CHAPTER TWO

Testing a Hypothesis

In the preceding chapter it was shown from Roman Catholic sources that, on the basis of that church's own interpretations, there seemed to be justification for the Protestant Reformers' identification of the pope and/or the papal system as the little horn of Daniel 7. But before accepting such a conclusion, fairness demands that further compelling evidence be adduced. Hence, in this chapter we will test the Reformers' accusations by comparing certain salient specifications of the prophecy of Daniel 7 with statements derived from Roman Catholic authorities and confirmed by non-Catholic sources.

According to Daniel 7:20 (NKJV), the "different" little-horn king was to become "greater than his fellows"—in other words, greater than the barbarian kingdoms that parceled out the Western Roman Empire. Did the papal system fulfill this specification? If so, how did it come about?

Greater than its fellows

Father Turmel, previously quoted, asks the following questions concerning the downfall of the Western Roman Empire and the rise of the papacy, then answers his own questions:

What is to become of the church? Are its days numbered, and is the Empire to bring it down as its companion into an open tomb?

No, the Church will not descend into the tomb. It will survive the Empire. It will have to pass through days of distress. It will witness calamity after calamity, ruins heaped upon ruins. But in the midst of the greatest sadness, it will receive precious consolations. One after another, these barbarian peoples will submit to its laws and will count it a glory to be the Church's children. The frontiers of the Church will be extended; its institutions, for a moment shaken by the Barbarians, will be consolidated, developed, and will adapt themselves to their surroundings. *The papacy,* most sorely tried of all, *will make a new advance. At length a second empire will arise, and of this empire the Pope will be the master—more than this, he will be the master of Europe.*[1]

So, the papacy rose to dominance *after* the barbarian kingdoms of northern Europe parceled out the Western Roman Empire. This confirms what the *New Catholic Encyclopedia,* quoted in chapter 1, implies (see page 11 above).

Carl Eckhardt, late professor of history at the University of Colorado, further confirms Turmel's assessment that the papacy grew out of the Roman Empire. Says he:

> Under the Roman Empire the popes had no temporal powers. But when the Roman Empire had disintegrated and its place had been taken by a number of rude, barbarous kingdoms, the Roman Catholic Church not only became independent of the states in religious affairs but also dominated secular affairs as well.[2]

The Reformers believed that they saw in the rise of the papacy, beginning with the laying low of the last of the three barbarian kingdoms in 538, a clear fulfillment of the prophecy of Daniel 7. But what about the little horn speaking arrogantly against the Most High? Has the papal system fulfilled this specification of Daniel's prophecy?

Speaks against the Most High

The reader is free to draw his own conclusion as to whether or not the papal system's professions quoted below fulfill the specifications of Daniel 7:8, 11, 20, 25 concerning the claims of the "little horn."

In his encyclical of June 20, 1894, Pope Leo XIII declared: "We hold upon this earth the place of God Almighty."[3]

Eighteenth-century canonist and consultor to the Congregation to the Holy Office (the Inquisition department of the Roman Curia), P. F. Lucius Ferraris asserted: "The pope . . . acts in the place of God upon earth."[4]

Alphonsus Maria de Liguori, reputed to be one of the greatest Catholic writers of the eighteenth century, makes the following claim with respect to the priests—and it goes without saying that what is true of the priests is true of any member of the papal hierarchy, including the pope. Says Liguori:

> We find that in obedience to the words of his priests—*Hoc est corpus meum* [This is my body]—God himself descends on the altar, that he comes whenever they call him, and as often as they call him, and places himself in their hands, *even though they should be his enemies.*[5]

What a startling declaration! God is *obliged* to descend from heaven *in obedience* to a priest's words even when that priest is an enemy of God! If this does not put Rome's sacerdotal system above God, what would?

But perhaps the following Roman Catholic source summarizes and corroborates most clearly the claim that the papal system, from priest to pope, is above God:

OPEN SECRETS OF THE ANTICHRIST

We ecclesiastics are as far above governments, emperors, kings, and princes of this world as is heaven above the earth. Earthly kings and princes are as different from the priests as is lead from the finest and purest gold. **Far below the priest are the angels and archangels**, because he can in God's name forgive sins, whereas the angels never could. We are superior to the mother of God, since **she gave Christ birth only once, and we create him all the time.** Yes, the priests are in a certain sense even **above God**, inasmuch as **He must be at all times and everywhere at our disposal**, and at our command come down from heaven for the consecration of the mass. God, it is true, created the world with the simple word "be," but **we priests create God Himself with three [four?] little words.**[6]

Whether or not such claims are arrogant we leave for the reader to judge, but one thing is certain, these claims are at least reminiscent of the claims of "the Man of Sin" of 2 Thessalonians 2:3, 4, who "EXALTS HIMSELF AGAINST ALL that is called God, or that is worshipped."[7] What other religious system in all history has declared itself to be above God? Even Lucifer only aspired to equality with God. (See Isa. 14:12, 13.)

Interestingly, in a footnote in his New Testament translation, from which the text in the previous paragraph was quoted, Roman Catholic Father Francis Aloysius Spencer says of the words "proclaiming himself to be God": "These words are understood of Antichrist."

According to Roman Catholic sources, Antichrist exalts himself above all that is called God or that is worshiped. What is one to conclude? If Antichrist was to exalt himself above all that is called God, and the claims of Roman Catholic authorities are that the papal hierarchy, from priests to pope, is above God, is this not a case of self-incrimination, irrespective of what the Protestant Reformers may have charged or claimed? To borrow a phrase from Job, "Your own mouth condemns you."[8]

Testing a Hypothesis

Bear in mind that the Bible is not speaking about an individual. *It is talking about a religious system—a succession of religio-political rulers with but a single head governing it at any given time.* But before jumping to conclusions: Is there any other evidence showing that the Protestant Reformers were justified in identifying the papal system as the little horn of Daniel 7?

There is!

A persecuting power

The prophecy of Daniel 7:25 predicts that the little horn would persecute. The Reformers claimed that the papal persecution of non-conforming Christians, whom the papacy considered "heretics," fulfilled this specification of the prophecy. Is the charge true?

Here is a candid statement, not from some medieval source, but from Father Alexius Lepicier, a Roman Catholic prelate, writing around the turn of the twentieth century:

> He who publicly avows a heresy and tries to pervert others by word or example, speaking absolutely, can not only be excommunicated but *even justly put to death*, lest he ruin others by pestilential contagion; for a bad man is worse than a wild beast, and does more harm.[9]

Whether or not Lepicier reflected official papal policy in making this statement is beside the point. The fact remains that, although at present the papacy does not persecute, it cannot be denied that in past ages it has persecuted to death people who dissented from its teachings. To his credit, in 1999 Pope John Paul II tacitly acknowledged that this was true.

Roman Catholic scholars Thomas and Gertrude Sartory have pointedly declared that

> no religion in the world (not a single one in the history of mankind) has on its conscience so many millions of people who

thought differently, believed differently. [Roman Catholic] Christianity is the most murderous religion there has ever been.[10]

William Lecky, Irish historian and member of the British Academy and French Institute, agrees with the Sartorys. He says:

> That the Church of Rome has shed more innocent blood than any other institution that has ever existed among mankind, will be questioned by no Protestant who has a competent knowledge of history.[11]

Churchmen excuse these enormities, claiming that those who committed them had good intentions—the salvation of those they tortured and whose lives they took. But it must be pointed out that attributing good motives to those who committed such atrocities sounds strangely like the fulfillment of Jesus' words, that the time would come when those who killed His followers—Christians—*would "think they . . . [were] doing God a service"* (John 16:2, CLB; emphasis supplied).

Changes feast days and the law

Another specification of the prophecy of Daniel 7 describes the little-horn king as "thinking to change the feast days and the law." The Aramaic word translated "law" is not *torah,* but *dawth,* God's Ten-Commandment law. People have the authority to change laws people have made—but not God's law. The question then is: Has the papal system thought it had the authority to change God's law? Here are some papal claims bearing on this point.

Lucius Ferraris, previously quoted, wrote in 1772: "The pope is of so great authority and power that he can *modify,* explain, or interpret *even divine laws.*"[12]

In support of this claim, Ferraris quotes Petrus de Ancharano, a fifteenth-century canonist and professor of jurisprudence in the university of Siena, who declared: "The Pope can *modify divine law,* since his power is not of man but of God, and he acts in the place of God upon earth, with the fullest power of binding and loosing his sheep."[13]

Has the papacy ever attempted to exercise this supposed authority to alter God's law?

A comparison of the ten commandments in certain catechisms with the Ten Commandments recorded in Exodus 20:3-17, in any Catholic (or for that matter, Protestant) translation of the Bible reveals such an attempt at a change. In those catechisms the second commandment, which forbids the worship of images, is omitted and Sunday is substituted for the seventh-day (Saturday) Sabbath specified by the fourth commandment.[14] The omission of the second commandment reduces the number of commandments to nine. So, to preserve the well-known number ten, some catechisms divide the tenth commandment in two. Does this not constitute "thinking to change the times [changing the Sabbath to Sunday] and the law [omitting the second commandment and dividing the tenth commandment in two]"? (See examples of papal tampering with God's Ten-Commandment law in endnote 13 at the close of this chapter.)

The papacy's predicament

Because the evidence supporting the Protestant Reformers' indictment of the papal system was so utterly damning, John Henry (Cardinal) Newman, felt obliged to write the following defense of his adopted church*:

> All the offices, names, honours, powers which it [the Church] claims depend upon the determination of the simple question— Has Christ or has He not left a representative behind Him?
>
> Now if He has, then all is easy and intelligible; this is what churchmen maintain; they welcome the news; and they recognize in the Church's acts but the fulfillment of the high trust

---

*Newman was an Anglican churchman who converted to Roman Catholicism in 1845.

committed to her. But let us suppose for a moment the other side of the alternative to be true;—supposing Christ has left no representative behind Him. Well then, here is a society which professes to take His place without warrant. It comes forward instead of Christ and for Him; it speaks for Him, it developes [*sic*] His words; it suspends His appointments, it grants dispensation in matters of positive duty; it professes to dispense grace, it absolves from sin;—and all this of its own authority. Is it not forthwith according to the very force of the word "Antichrist?" He who speaks for Christ must be either His true servant or Antichrist; and nothing but Antichrist can he be, if appointed servant there is none. Let his acts be the same in both cases, according as he has authority or not, so is he most holy or most guilty. It is not the acts that make the difference, it is the *authority* for those acts. The very same acts are Christ's acts or Antichrist's, according to the doer: They are Christ's if Christ does them; they are Antichrist's if Christ does them not. There is no medium [middle ground] between a Vice-Christ and Antichrist."[15]

Similarly, Henry Edward (Cardinal) Manning, another Anglican churchman who also converted to Catholicism, wrote of the Catholic Church:

Now a system like this [the Roman Catholic Church] is so unlike anything human, it has upon it notes, tokens, marks so altogether supernatural, that men now acknowledge it to be either Christ or Antichrist. There is nothing between these extremes. Most true is this alternative. The Catholic Church is either the masterpiece of Satan or the kingdom of the Son of God.[16]

In the two declarations just quoted members of the papal hierarchy put the issue squarely on the line. The reader is free to draw his own conclusion as to which of the two alternatives is the most compelling.

Testing a Hypothesis

Preterism and futurism

The Protestant Reformers presented evidence that the papal system fulfilled the specifications of the little horn of Daniel 7. We believe that at the very least the two apologies quoted above reveal the extremely vulnerable position in which this evidence placed the Roman Catholic Church. Hence, the papacy was forced to find a way out. So, the pope convened the Council of Trent, which met off and on for eighteen years (1545-1563). One of the main purposes of this conventicle was to search for ways to sidestep the Reformers' accusation that the papal system was the little Antichristian horn of Daniel 7.

Following the Tridentine Council, two Jesuit priests devised diametrically opposite systems of interpretation, both of which attempted to turn the accusing finger of prophecy away from the papacy. One system pushed the three-and-a-half times of little-horn dominance back into the past, before the popes ruled Rome. The other shoved the three-and-a-half years forward into the dim and distant future. Either interpretation, *if true,* would free the papacy from the charge that it was the little horn power of Daniel 7—*a charge that interpreters of the prophecies, both Catholic and Protestant, had expressed in earlier times.*

The Catholic writer George S. Hitchcock frankly tells us who devised these conflicting systems of interpretation. He says:

> The Futuristic School, founded by the Jesuit [Francisco] Ribera in 1591, looks for Antichrist, Babylon, and a rebuilt temple in Jerusalem, at the end of the Christian Dispensation.
> The Praeterist School, founded by the Jesuit [Luis de] Alcasar in 1614, explains the Revelation by the Fall of Jerusalem, or by the fall of Pagan Rome in 410 A.D. [sic].[17]

Joseph Tanner, a Protestant writer of the nineteenth century, confirms what Hitchcock says—and explains *why* the papacy did what it did. He wrote:

Towards the close of the century of the Reformation, two of her [the Catholic Church's] most learned doctors set themselves to the task [of reinterpreting prophecy], each endeavoring . . . to [divert] men's minds from perceiving the fulfillment of the prophecies of the antichrist in the papal system. The Jesuit Alcasar devoted himself to bring into prominence the *Preterist* method of interpretation . . . [by endeavoring to show] that the prophecies of antichrist were fulfilled before the popes ever ruled at Rome, and therefore could not apply to the papacy. On the other hand the Jesuit Ribera tried to set aside the application of these prophecies to the papal power by bringing out the *Futurist* system, which asserts that these prophecies refer properly not to the career of the Papacy, but to that of some future supernatural individual, who is yet to appear to continue in power for three and a half years. Thus, as [Dean Henry] Alford [the noted British scholar] says, the Jesuit Ribera, about 1580, may be regarded as the founder of the Futurist system in modern times.[18]

Tanner then laments:

It is a matter for deep regret that those who hold and advocate the Futurist system at the present day, Protestants as they are for the most part, are thus really playing into the hands of Rome, and helping to screen the papacy from detection as the antichrist.[19]

Is it not ironic that the spiritual descendants of the Protestant Reformers, evangelical Protestants, whether wittingly or unwittingly, turn out to be the chief defenders of the papacy today? How did this happen? Copies of the prophetic works of Ribera and Alcasar (also spelled Alcazar) lay dormant in the universities of Europe for more than two centuries. Then, around 1830, the Plymouth Brethren began studying these interpretations and adopted futurism. Soon, other denominations began incorporating these interpretations into their prophetic views: The liberal, higher critical wing of Protestantism adopted Alcazar's preterism, and conservative Protestants adopted Ribera's futurism.[20]

In 1909, futurism was given a tremendous boost when Dr. Cyrus I. Scofield introduced it into the footnotes of many Protestant Bibles.[21] It has since become the generally accepted system of interpretation of Protestant Fundamentalists and Evangelicals and is the basis of Dispensationalism and the Rapture Theory.

What about the "year, two years, and a half-year" of little horn ascendancy? Does it fit the period of papal domination of Christendom? The Protestant Reformers held that it did, and some post-Reformation Protestants believed that the three-and-a-half times/ years of papal ascendancy began in A.D. 538 and ended 1,260 years later, in 1798. Both Preterists and Futurists challenge the validity of this interpretation, insisting that "a time, times, and a division of a time" amount to three-and-a-half literal years and therefore cannot fit the period of papal dominance. Hence, the prophecy could not apply to the papal system.

We shall examine this objection in the next chapter.

---

1. Lagard, *op. cit.*, v, vi. Quoted in *Bible Students' Source Book,* 690. Emphasis supplied.
2. Carl Conrad Eckhardt, *The Papacy in World-Affairs* (Chicago: The University of Chicago Press, 1937), 1. Quoted in *Bible Students' Source Book,* 694.
3. Pope Leo XIII. Encyclical Letter, "The Reunion of Christendom," dated June 20, 1894, translated in *The Great Encyclical Letters of Leo XIII* (New York: Benziger, 1903), 304. Quoted in *Source Book,* 684.
4. P. F. Lucius Ferraris, *Prompta bibliotheca canonica juridica, moralis, theologica nec non ascetica, polemica, rubricistica, historica* ("Handy Library" etc., abbreviated *Prompta bibliotheca*), p. 29, art. 2, "Papa" (Venentiis [Venice]: Gaspar Storti, 1772; rev., Rome: Press of the Propaganda, 1899). Quoted in *Bible Students' Source Book,* 680.
5. St. Alphonsus de Liguori, *Dignities and Duties of the Priest, or Selva* (Brooklyn: Redemptorist Fathers, 1927), 26. *Nihil obstat.* Arthur J. Scanlan, S.T.D., *Censor Librorum. Imprimature.* Patritius Cardinalis Hayes, Archiepiscopus Neo-Eboracensis. Neo-Eboraci [New York,] Die 24 Mar., 1927. Emphasis supplied.
6. *Norddeutsche Zeitung,* No. 21, 1872. Quoted by Ruy Barbosa in a footnote in the foreword *O Papa e o Concilio,* a trans. of *The Pope and the Council,* by Janus (pseudonym for Dr.

Johann Joseph Ignaz von Döllinger) (São Paulo: Saraiva & Cia, 2 edição, 1930), 114. Bold emphasis in Barbosa's original. The paragraph reads as follows in the Portuguese translation:

Estamos os ecclesiasticos tanto ácima dos governos, imperadores, reis e principes deste mundo quanto o céu ácima da terra. Os reis e principes mundanos diferencêam-se tanto dos padres, quanto o chumbo do oiro mais fino e mais puro. **Muito abaixo do padre estão os anjos e archanjos:** porque elle pode em nome de Deus perdoar os pecados ao passo que os anjos nunca o puderam. Nós somos superiores á mãe de Deus; porquanto ella **não deu á luz o Christo senão uma só vez, e nós o creamos todo dia.** Sim, os sacerdotes estão, até de certo modo **ácima de Deus;** visto que **elle deve achar-se, a todo tempo e em toda parte, á nossa disposição,** e por ordem nossa baixar do céu para a consagração da missa. Deus creou, é certo, o mundo com a simples palavra "seja," **mas nós, padres, creamos o proprio Deus com tres** [quatro?] **palavrinhas** [hoc est corpus meum]. (Enfase Barbosa.)

Although attempts were made to obtain this statement in German from its original source, these attempts were not successful, and this researcher apologizes for having to translate the statement from Portuguese into English. Donald E. Mansell, translator.

7. *The New Testament of Our Lord and Saviour Jesus Christ,* Francis Aloysius Spencer, O.P., trans.; Charles J. Callan, O.P. and John A. McHugh, O.P., eds. (New York: The Macmillan Company, 1937). IMPRIMI PERMITTIMUS: Fr. M. S. Gillet, O.P., *Magister Generalis;* IMPRIMI POTEST: Fr. T. S. McDermott, O.P., S.T.Lr., *Provincialis;* NIHIL OBSTAT: Arthur J. Scanlan, S.T.D., *Censor Librorum;* IMPRIMATUR: Patrick Cardinal Hayes, *Archbishop of New York.* New York, June 17, 1937. Capital letters his.

8. *The New Jerusalem Bible* (NJB).

9. Fr. Alexius M. Lepicier, O.S.M., *De Stabilitate et Progresser Dogmatis* (Rome: Printed at the official printing office, 1910), 194. Quoted by Frank H. Yost in *Our Firm Foundation* (Washington, D.C.: Review and Herald Publishing Association, 1953), 1:704. Emphasis supplied.

10. Thomas and Gertrude Sartory, *In der Hölle Brennt Kein Feuer* (Munich: 1968), 88, 89; quoted by H. Kung, *Eternal Life?* (Garden City, New York: Doubleday, 1984), 132. See *Symposium on Revelation: Exegetical and General Studies* (Silver Spring, Md.: Biblical Research Institute, General Conference of Seventh-day Adventists, 1992), 7:2:169.

11. W[illiam] E[dward] H[artpole] Lecky, *History of the Rise and Influence of the Spirit of Rationalism in Europe* (reprint; New York: Braziller, 1955), 2:40.

12. Ferraris, *op. cit.,* art. "Papa," p. 29. Latin. Quoted in *Bible Students' Source Book,* 680. Emphasis supplied.

13. Ibid.

14. "Q. *Which is the Sabbath day?*

"A. Saturday is the Sabbath day.

"Q. *Why do we observe Sunday instead of Saturday?*

"A. We observe Sunday instead of Saturday because the Catholic Church transferred the solemnity from Saturday to Sunday."—Peter Geiermann, C.SS.R., *The Convert's Catechism of Catholic Doctrine* (St. Louis: Missouri: B. Herder Book Co., 1930, 1957), 48-55. This catechism has no NIHIL OBSTAT; however, it did receive the apostolic blessing of Pope Pius X on January 25, 1910. IMPRIMATUR: Joseph E. Ritter, S.T.D., Archbishop of St. Louis. September 16, 1957. Quoted in *Bible Students' Source Book,* 886. Cf. Dan. 7:25 in any Roman Catholic-approved translation of the Scriptures.

Testing a Hypothesis

"*Q. Have you any other way of proving that the Church has power to institute festivals of precept?*

"A. Had she not such power, she could not have done that in which all modern religionists agree with her:—she could not have substituted the observance of Sunday the first day of the week, for the observance of Saturday the seventh day, a change for which there is no Scriptural authority."—Stephen B. Keenan, *A Doctrinal Catechism* (New York: T. W. Strong, late Edward Dunnigan & Bro., 1876, 3rd American ed. rev.), p. 174 Quoted in *Bible Students' Source Book,* 886.

Bertrand L. Conway claims that the Roman Catholic Church had the authority to transfer the observance of the Sabbath to Sunday. However, he concedes that "if the Bible is the only guide for the Christian, then the Seventh Day Adventist [sic] is right in observing the Saturday with the Jew." Bertrand L. Conway, *The Question Box Answers* (New York: The Columbus Press, 1910), 254. An article in "The Question Box" (*The Catholic Universe Bulletin,* 69 [Aug. 14, 1942], 4) maintains that the Roman Catholic Church had the "divine right" to change "the observance from Sabbath to Sunday." It continues, "The Protestant, claiming the Bible to be the only guide of faith, has no warrant for observing Sunday. In this matter the Seventh Day Adventist [sic] is the only consistent Protestant."

15. John Henry (Cardinal) Newman, "The Protestant Idea of Antichrist," *The British Critic and Quarterly Theological Review,* no. 28 (October 1840), 431, 432. Quoted in *Bible Students' Source Book,* 36. Emphasis Newman's.

16. Henry Edward (Cardinal) [Manning], *The Fourfold Sovereignty of God* (London: Burns, Oates, and Company, 1871), 170, 171. Author identified in the British Museum Catalog. Quoted by Froom in *Prophetic Faith,* 3:737, 774.

17. George S. Hitchcock, *The Beasts and the Little Horn* (London: Catholic Truth Society Publications, 1911), 7. Quoted by Froom in *Prophetic Faith,* 2:488.

18. Joseph Tanner, *Daniel and the Revelation* (London: Hodder and Stoughton, 1898), 16, 17. Quoted by J. H. Meier, *What Catholics and Protestants Should Know* (Nampa, Idaho: Pacific Press Publishing Association, 1953), 159.

19. Ibid.

20. *Prophetic Faith,* vol. 2, chapters 22 and 23.

21. *The New Scofield Study Bible* (New York: Oxford University Press, 1967), v-ix.

CHAPTER THREE

The Duration of "Little-Horn" Dominance

Expositors of Bible prophecy are usually divided into three major schools of interpretation, the first two of which have already been mentioned: 1) The preterist school, which finds the fulfillment of prophecy close to the prophet's own day,* 2) the futurist school, which sees much of prophecy fulfilled in a remote age to come, and 3) the historicist school, which sees prophecy fulfilling in a progressive, continuous, unbroken sequence from the prophet's day down to the end of the age. The Protestant Reformers belonged to the latter school of interpretation, and so did some Roman Catholics, as has been shown in the previous chapters.

Scholars of all three schools agree that, in the expression that literally reads, "a time, times, and the division of a time," the word "time" means a year.[1] This is common ground. However, both preterists and futurists understand the sum of these periods to be 1,260 days or three-and-a-half literal years, while historicists interpret it to stand for 1,260 symbolic days or 1,260 natural—that is, solar—years.

---

*The historical-critical school holds a similar view, hence I have included it with the preterists.

The Duration of "Little-Horn" Dominance

How did these schools of interpretation arrive at such divergent conclusions, and which school is correct?

"Times" equals "years"

Before answering this question, let us begin with the common ground: "times" in Daniel 7:25 means "years."

As pointed out above, the time period mentioned in Daniel 7:25 literally reads, "a time, times, and a division of a time" (Young). In Daniel 12:7 this period is called "a time, times, and half a time," so "a division of a time" is simply another way of saying "half a time." Most translations render it this way. The expression "a time, times, and half a time" is also found in Revelation 12:14 (D-R). But now notice. In verse 6 of that chapter this time period is equated with "a thousand two hundred and sixty days."

Revelation 11:3 (D-R) also contains the expression "a thousand two hundred and sixty days," which the preceding verse equates with "two and forty months." Forty-two months, of course, is three-and-a-half years. So, "a time, times, and half a time" stands for 1,260 days. A footnote on Revelation 11:2 in the Catholic- and Protestant-approved *New Oxford Annotated Revised Standard Version* sums up and confirms this conclusion, putting it simply "Forty-two months = 1260 days = 3 1/2 years (Dan. 7:25; 12:7)."[2] Bible students unanimously agree with this synchronization.

Does this expression, then, represent three-and-a-half literal years, as preterists and futurists claim, or 1,260 years, as the Protestant Reformers claimed?

At first blush one might think that the preterist/futurist interpretation that the three-and-a-half times represents literal years is the better explication of the expression than is the historicists' 1,260 solar years. However, technically, three-and-a-half literal years equal 1278.375+ days, *not* 1260 days.* This disparity strongly suggests that the three-and-a-

---

* 365.25+ X 3.5 = 1278.375+

half years are *not* to be understood as years of 365.25+ days each. Yet, this is not the most serious objection to the futurist/preterist interpretations concerning this time period.

The expression "a time, times, and a division of a time" is not the usual way of saying three-and-a-half literal years. This peculiarity, plus the fact that much of the book of Daniel is clearly symbolic, suggests that this expression has a cryptic meaning.

How do historicists decipher the "cryptogram"? How do "a time, times, and half a time" equal 1,260 solar years?

1,260 solar years

Many conservative Bible scholars, both Catholic and Protestant, agree that the prophecy of Daniel 9:25 is a prediction about the Messiah.[3] This prophecy says that "from the going forth of the word to build up Jerusalem again, unto Christ the prince, there shall be seven weeks and sixty-two weeks" (D-R). The Douay-Rheims Version interprets this to mean that, from a starting point sometime during the Medo-Persian period (539 to 323 B.C.), a span of 483 years would extend "to the baptism of Christ, when he first began to preach and execute the office of Messias."[4] So, we see that conservative Catholic and Protestant scholars understand that a prophetic day represents a solar year, *at least in the prophecy of Daniel 9.*

Is this interpretation of a day for a year far-fetched? No. Numerous Bible versions and translations render the expression "seventy weeks" in verse 24 as "seventy weeks of *years.*"* When Daniel wishes to differentiate between ordinary weeks and prophetic weeks, he uses the expression "weeks of days"[5] to refer to the former.

So certain is Roman Catholic scholar Monsignor Ronald Knox that the weeks of Daniel 9:24 are weeks of years, not weeks of seven days that he says in a footnote on verse 27 in his translation of the Bible:

---

*Emphasis supplied. See, e.g., RSV, CLB, GNB, Revised English Bible (REB), Smith-Goodspeed (S-G), Amplified, etc. Justification for this translation will be discussed in chapter 6.

Modern commentators, who understand the whole passage [Dan. 9:24-27] as a reference to Antiochus Epiphanes, and the profanation of the Temple in B.C. 167, are driven to *very unconvincing explanations* of the time periods involved.[6]

Historicists could not agree more!

Clearly, Msgr. Knox rejects the interpretation that the time periods of Daniel 9 signify literal time. Instead, he holds the historicist view that a day stands for a solar year in this Messianic prophecy.

One thing is certain, 483 years* from the seventh year of the reign of Artaxerxes—which turns out to be 457 B.C.,[7] as will be shown—until Jesus' baptism, at which time He began to exercise His role as Messiah, fits the prophetic time period with undeniable accuracy. This agrees with Jesus' announcement at the beginning of His Galilean ministry that "the time is fulfilled" (Mark 1:15). Clearly, Jesus was referring to the time prophecy of Daniel 9 (cp. Gal. 4:4).

If a day stands for a year in Daniel 9:24-27, it seems reasonable to assume that the same principle applies to the expression "time, times, and the dividing of time" (= 3 1/2 years = 42 months = 1,260 days).[†] If this is correct, 1,260 prophetic days stand for 1,260 solar years.

Does the Bible anywhere explicitly state that a day stands for a year in Bible prophecy? *It does!*

In the prophecy of the siege of Jerusalem, God told Ezekiel, "A day for a year, I have appointed to thee" (Ezek. 4:6, D-R). And Numbers 14:34 (NJB), says, "Each day shall count for a year."

Since God is the One who set forth the principle that a day stands for a solar year in the time prophecies of Numbers and Ezekiel, it seems only natural that He would employ the same principle in all the time prophecies of Daniel. Thus, the day-for-a-year principle is not some

---

* 7 + 62 x 7 = 483.
† See the summary in Rev. 11:2, RSV above, p. 31.

far-fetched idea dreamed up by Protestant historicists to condemn the papacy. It has a divine precedent.

Does the period of 1,260 years, when applied to the prophecy of the little horn, fit naturally into the period of papal dominance? *It does!*

The little horn's ascendancy

In chapter 1 it was shown that the last of the "hindering horns," the Ostrogothic kingdom, was not laid low until A.D. 538. Consequently, *the little horn could not begin to become "greater than his fellows" prior to 538.* Justinian, emperor of the Eastern Roman Empire, issued the "Decretum Iustinianum" in 533, addressing Pope John II as "the most Holy Archbishop and Patriarch of the noble city of Rome." In this imperial rescript, Justinian decreed that the pope should be "the head of all the churches."[8] However, Justinian's decree could not be implemented until March 538, when the Ostrogoths were driven from the city of Rome. So, 538 is the logical date from which to begin the 1,260 years of papal ascendancy.

If this is true, the 1,260 years must have terminated around the end of February 1798.*

Did it? *It did!*

The English Jesuit priest Joseph Rickaby wrote:

> When, in 1797, Pope Pius VI fell grievously ill, Napoleon [Bonaparte] gave orders that in the event of his [the Pope's] death no successor should be elected to his office, and that the Papacy should be discontinued.
>
> But the Pope recovered; the peace was soon broken; [General Pierre Alexandre] Berthier entered Rome on [the] 10th [of] February 1798, and proclaimed a Republic. The aged Pontiff refused to violate his oath by recognizing it, and was [escorted out of Rome on February 20th and] hurried from prison to prison

---

* 538 + 1260 = 1798.

in France. Broken with fatigue and sorrows, he died [on the 19ᵗʰ of] August, 1799, in the French fortress of Valence, aged 82 years. No wonder that half [of] Europe thought Napoleon's veto would be obeyed, and that with the Pope the Papacy was dead.[10]

Speaking of this crushing blow to the papacy, George Trevor, Anglican clergyman and canon of York, confirmed Rickaby's candid assessment of what happened at the end of February 1798. He said:

> The Papacy was extinct: not a vestige of its existence remained; and among all the Roman Catholic powers not a finger was stirred in its defense. The Eternal City had no longer prince or pontiff; its bishop was a dying captive in foreign lands; and the decree was already announced that no successor would be allowed in his place.[11]

Although a new pope, Pius VII, was elected shortly, in 1800, the heyday of the papacy was over—*for the time being.* Since 1798, the papacy has not enjoyed the power it exercised in Christendom for the greater part of thirteen centuries. The fact that it has survived and seems to be experiencing a revival is part of the prophecy of Revelation 13.

In his book *The Keys of This Blood* Malachi Martin writes of the decline in papal fortunes since 1798 and then laments that "two hundred years of inactivity had been imposed on the papacy by the major secular powers of the world."[12] However, if we may be pardoned for a play on words, Martin "vaticinates"* (that is, "forecasts"), that this situation will change—a prediction that is in perfect agreement with the prophecy of Revelation 13:1-17, especially verse 3. (Notice that the

---

* *Vaticinate,* from *mons* or *collis Vaticanus,* the hill of the soothsayers or "prophets" of the ancient city of Rome.

first beast portrayed in this chapter incorporates salient characteristics of the four beasts of Daniel 7—*and in addition speaks great words against the Most High [Rev. 13:5, 6], identifying it as the little horn of Daniel 7.* John said that it would receive a mortal wound and then recover from that wound.)

End of the 1,260 years

In 1689, more than a century before the termination of the 1,260 years, Drue Cressener, an Anglican cleric and student of Bible prophecy, on the basis of the prophecies of Daniel 7 and Revelation 13, made the following "uncanny" prediction: "The first appearance of the Beast was at *Justinian's* recovery of the Western Empire, from which time to about the year 1800 will be about 1,260 years."[13]

On the next page of his book, Cressener is even more precise. He says that this period will end "a little before the year 1800." *It ended in late February 1798—exactly 1,260 years from the time the Ostrogothic "horn" was laid low and driven from the city of Rome in March 538!*

When the little horn became ascendant in 538, the popes, for all intents and purposes, became the emperors of the Western Roman Empire. This is no strained interpretation invented by the Protestant Reformers to condemn Catholics. *Roman Catholic authorities acknowledge that the papal system is a continuation of the Roman Empire in religious garb.* For instance, the Catholic priest James P. Conroy wrote:

> Long ages ago, when Rome through the neglect of the Western emperors was left to the mercy of the barbarous hordes [the Germanic tribes], the Romans turned to one figure for aid and protection, and asked him to rule them; and thus, in this simple manner, the best title of all to kingly right, commenced the temporal sovereignty of the popes. And meekly *stepping to the throne of Caesar,* the vicar of Christ took up the scepter to which the emperors and kings of Europe were to bow in reverence through so many ages.[14]

The Duration of "Little-Horn" Dominance

In *The Keys of This Blood,* Malachi Martin speaks of the Roman Catholic Church as wearing "a regal but ill-fitting cloak from the ancient Romans"[15]—his way of saying that the popes are the successors of the Roman emperors. And Alexander Flick, late professor of European history at Syracuse University, said the same thing as Conroy and Martin. He wrote:

> The papal theory . . . made the Pope alone God's representative on earth and maintained that the Emperor received his right to rule from St. Peter's successor. . . . It was upheld by Nicholas I, Hildebrand, Alexander III, Innocent III, and culminated with Boniface VIII at the jubilee of 1300 when, seated on the throne of Constantine, girded with the imperial sword, wearing a crown, and waving a sceptre, he shouted to the throng of loyal pilgrims: "*I am Caesar—I am Emperor.*"[16]

In this connection, note that the pagan Roman beast was to continue on in the papal little horn. This is why Daniel 7:11 doesn't speak of the destruction of the little horn, but rather says, "The *beast* [from which the little horn grew] was killed, and its body destroyed and committed to the flames" (v. 11, JB). This clearly implies that the little horn is in effect a continuation of the Roman Empire—*with religious overtones to be sure.* And this, *by its own claims,* is what the papal succession professes to be.

In previous chapters, we quoted papal authorities who identify the little horn with Antichrist. Other papal authorities identify "the man of sin" of 2 Thessalonians 2:3-8 with Antichrist.[17] So, according to these authorities, both passages are speaking of Antichrist.

Now notice: 2 Thessalonians 2:3, 8 states that Christ will "destroy"

---

*Remember, the Antichrist *"shall think to change times and the law"*! (Dan. 7:25, RSV; emphasis supplied).

"the man of lawlessness" with the breath of his mouth and . . . by his appearing and his coming" (RSV). This clearly indicates that Antichrist is to continue until the Second Advent, when he will be destroyed. 2 Thessalonians 1:8 says he will be destroyed "in blazing fire"[18] (NAB) or by the "flaming fire" (RSV) of Christ's coming (cp. Rev. 19:11-21). Speaking of the destruction of the Roman beast and its little horn, Daniel 7:9-11 says:

> As I looked,
>   thrones were placed
> and one that was ancient of days took his seat;
>   his raiment was white as snow,
> and the hair of his head like pure wool;
>   his throne was fiery flames,
> its wheels were burning fire.
>   A stream of fire issued
> and came forth from before him;
>   a thousand thousands served him,
> and ten thousand times ten thousand stood before him;
>   the court sat in judgment,
> and the books were opened.
> I looked then because of the sound of the great words which the horn was speaking. And as I looked, *the beast was slain, and its body destroyed and given over to be burned with fire* (RSV; emphasis supplied).

The conclusion appears inescapable: *The Roman beast is annihilated with the little horn at the Second Coming.* And Revelation 19:11-20 confirms this conclusion. (See Rev. 13: 1, 2, 11-14 for the identity of the beast and the false prophet.)

Notice also that, according to Daniel 7:10, 11, before Christ returns "in flaming fire" and destroys the beast, the little horn is heard boasting. Interestingly, as the evidence in chapter 2 shows, some of the most extravagant claims the papal system has uttered have been made *since 1844—while, as will now be shown, the pre-Advent judgment of Daniel 7:10 is going on!*

The judgment scene described in Daniel 7:9-11 is obviously not the judgment described in Revelation 20, when all those whose names are not found written in the book of life personally appear before the Judge of all the earth. The late Arno C. Gaebelein—not a Seventh-day Adventist, but an Evangelical Protestant—declared emphatically that these judgments are separate and distinct. He stated that, "This judgment [the judgment of Daniel 7:9, 10] is not the last judgment at all. It is a judgment which precedes the final judgment by 1,000 years."[19]

Unlike the great white throne judgment, this pre-millennial judgment is conducted on the basis of record books, not personal appearance (see Daniel 7:10). It *precedes* the Second Advent and takes place in heaven.

Although someday "we must all appear before the judgment seat of Christ" (2 Corinthians 5:10, RSV), the judgment described in Daniel 7:9, 10 is conducted by the "Ancient of Days" (God the Father), not by the "one like the Son of man" (Christ), who is "brought near before him." In this judgment, we (God's professed people) do not appear personally. Rather, our records, the "books," are opened for inspection, and "the Son of Man," our "advocate with the Father" (1 John 2:1), appears before Him on our behalf.

Focus on the papal system

On the basis of Catholic interpretations, acknowledgments, and claims, all corroborated by the facts of history, what conclusion can one come to other than that the Protestant Reformers had compelling reasons for seeing in the *papal system* the fulfillment of the prophecy of the little horn of Daniel 7?

Does this mean that every Roman Catholic communicant is an antichrist? *No!* We are *not* discussing individuals but a *system*—the papal hierarchy, the papal succession. Many Catholics, and doubtless some popes, have been better Christians than many Protestants—Seventh-day Adventists not excepted. Neither does our conclusion mean that the papal system at the present time claims and practices that which it once claimed and practiced. On the other hand, it *does* mean that, except for *subscribing* to religious liberty[20] *at the present time,* the papal hierarchy has never officially renounced or repudiated its former practices and claims, nor has it ever promised that in the future it would not revive these claims and practices. *We believe prophecy predicts a revival of papal persecutions.*

In Revelation 13, the apostle John described a sea beast that incorporates the characteristics of the Babylonian lion, the Medo-Persian bear, the Grecian leopard, the terrible Roman beast, and the papal horn of the vision of Daniel 7. He said that the papal head "seemed to have been mortally wounded, but this mortal wound was healed" (Rev. 13:3, NAB). This suggests that the time would come when the papal power would receive a *seemingly* mortal blow, but would subsequently be revived. As previously shown, General Berthier administered the near-fatal blow in 1798, when he took Pope Pius VI captive. As a consequence, for the past two hundred years the papal system has not been able to exercise the power it once practiced.

But a change will come. In *The Keys of This Blood,* Martin envisions the revival of papal power not seen in the past two centuries. He foresees the time when the pope will announce at a consistory that he is *resuming the former authoritarian powers of the papacy.*[21]

Seventh-day Adventists agree that the papacy will experience a revival, but we envision a somewhat different revival scenario. We believe, on the basis of Revelation 13:11-17, that the *"second,"* or land, beast—Protestant America—will "breathe life into" the *"first,"* or papal, beast, which received the seemingly mortal wound (see Revelation 13:1, 11, 12, 15, NAB). We believe that the Protestants of the United States will be foremost in stretching their hands across the gulf to grasp the hand of Spiritualism; they will reach over the abyss to clasp hands with the Roman power; and under the influence of this threefold union, this country [the United States] will follow in the steps of Rome in trampling on the rights of conscience.[22]

Seventh-day Adventists believe that in the future, perhaps sooner than many think, Protestant America will unite with spiritualism and the papacy, and the latter's persecuting practices will be revived. At this writing (A.D. 2001), spiritualistic TV programs are sweeping America, while, at the same time, Protestants of the United States are making overtures for a union with Rome. When this threefold union is formed, the papacy will supply the leadership. ("Under one head—the papal power—the people will unite to oppose God in the person of His witnesses."[23]) Apostate Protestant America, the world's sole superpower, will supply the military might to enforce the dictates of the papacy. ("The beast with lamb-like horns [the United States government[24]] speaks with the voice of a dragon, and . . . will say 'to them that dwell on the earth, that they should make an image to the beast.' . . . the papacy."[25]) And spiritualism, the near-universal belief in the immortality of the soul, will supply the worldwide bond holding this threefold union together. ("This union is cemented by the great apostate [Satan, working through spiritualism]."[26])

However, the revival of papal power is not the end of the story. According to Daniel 7, the coming judgment has two aspects: 1) At the close of the pre-Advent assize, judgment is "pronounced *in favor* of the holy ones of the Most High" (vs. 21, 22, emphasis supplied). 2) Later, at the Second Coming, judgment is executed *against* the persecuting little horn (v. 11). We will continue to discuss this pre-Advent judgment in chapter 7 of this book.

1. Robert Young, *Young's Literal Translation of the Bible,* rev. ed. (Grand Rapids, Mich.: Baker Book House, 1956). Abbreviated Young.

2. *An Ecumenical Study Bible: The New Oxford Annotated Bible with the Apocrypha: Revised Standard Version,* Herbert G. May and Bruce M. Metzger, eds. (New York: Oxford University Press, 1977), footnote on Revelation 11:2. The dust cover says that it is "the first edition of the English Bible to receive both Protestant and Catholic approval." Abbreviated New Oxford Annotated RSV.

3. Gerhard F. Hasel, in *The Seventy Weeks, Leviticus, and the Nature of Prophecy,* Frank B. Holbrook, ed. (Washington, D.C.: Biblical Research Institute, 1986), 48, lists a score of scholars that hold or have held the historical Messianic interpretation of Daniel 9:24-27. Says Hasel, "There are still stout supporters of the Messianic interpretation to the present among both Catholic and Protestant scholars on both sides of the Atlantic." Chapter 1, footnote 96.

4. D-R, footnote on Dan. 9:25.

5. *The Interlinear Bible,* Jay P. Green, Sr., gen. ed. and trans. (Grand Rapids, Mich.: Baker Book House, 1976-1979, by Jay P. Green, Sr.), Daniel 10:2, marginal translation; p. 691.

6. *The Holy Bible,* Monsignor Ronald J. Knox, trans. (New York: Sheed & Ward, Inc., 1950), footnote on Daniel 9:27. No Nihil Obstat. Imprimatur: Bernardus (Cardinal) Griffin, Archiepiscopus Westmonasteriensis, Westmonasterii, die 8 Decembris 1954. Abbreviated Knox. Emphasis supplied.

7. Siegfried H. Horn and Lynn H. Wood, *The Chronology of Ezra 7* (Washington, D.C.: Review and Herald Publishing Association, 1970), 127. This detailed examination of the systems of calendars in use in the Middle East in the sixth century B.C. establishes beyond reasonable doubt that the seventh year of Artaxerxes was 458/457 B.C., not 459/458 B.C. as some have supposed.

8. *Codex Iustinianum,* lib. 1, title 1: "Annales Ecclesiastici," Caesar Baronio, Ann. 533, sec. 12; translation given in *The Petrine Claims,* R.F. Littledale (London: Society for Promoting Christian Knowledge, 1889), 293. Quoted in *Source Book for Bible Students* (Washington, D.C.: Review and Herald Publishing Association, 1922), 382, 383.

9. *Encyclopedia Britannica* (Chicago: Encyclopedia Britannica, Inc., 1954), art. "Pius VI," 17:982.

10. Joseph Rickaby, "The Modern Papacy," *Lectures on the History of Religions* (London: Catholic Truth Society, 1910), vol. 3, lecture 24, p. 1. Quoted in *Bible Students' Source Book,* 703.

11. George Trevor, *Rome: From the Fall of the Western Empire* (London: The Religious Tract Society, 1868), 440. Quoted in *Source Book,* 701.

12. Malachi Martin, *The Keys of This Blood,* (New York: Simon & Schuster, 1990), 22.

13. Drue Cressener, *The Judgments of God Upon the Roman Catholick Church* (London: Printed for Richard Chiswell, 1698), 309. Quoted by Froom in *Prophetic Faith,* 2:596. Emphasis his.

14. Rev. James P. Conroy, *American Catholic Quarterly Review,* April 1911. Quoted in *Source Book for Bible Students,* 388. Emphasis supplied.

15. Martin, 136.

16. Alexander Clarence Flick, *The Rise of the Mediaeval Church* (New York: Burt Franklin, [1959]), 413. Quoted in *Bible Students' Source Book,* 683. Emphasis supplied.

17. *The New Testament of Our Lord and Saviour Jesus Christ* (Paterson, New Jersey: St. Anthony Guild Press, 1941, Confraternity ed.), footnotes on 2 Thess. 2:3, 4, 7, 8, 9. *Nihil Obstat,* Rt. Rev. Msgr. Henry J. Grimmelsman, S.T.D.; Rev. John F. McConnell, M.M., S.T.L., S.S.L.; Rev. Joseph J. Tennant, S.T.D., S.S.L., *Imprimatur.* Most Rev. Thomas H. McLaughlin, S.T.C., Bishop of Paterson. Cp. *D-R,* footnote on 2 Thess. 2:3. Cp. also *The New Testament in the Westminster Version of the Sacred Scriptures,* Cuthbert Lattey, S.J., trans. (New York: Longmans, Green and Co., 1948), *Nihil Obstat.* Johannes M. T. Barton, S.T.D., L.S.S., Censor Deputatus. *Imprimatur.* E. Morrogh Bernard. Vic. Gen. Westmonasterii, die 26A Novembris, 1947. Sidehead for 2 Thessalonians ch. 2 and footnote on v. 8. Cp. also Spencer, *The New Testament.* Footnote on 2 Thess. 2:4.

18. *The Catholic Study Bible: New American Bible,* Donald Senior, gen. ed. (New York: Oxford University Press, 1990). *Nihil Obstat:* Reverend John G. Lodge, S.T.L., S.S.L.; Reverend Robert L. Shoenstene, M.A., S.S.L., Censor Deputatis. *Imprimatur:* Reverend P. Roache, Vicar General, Archdiocese of Chicago, November 27, 1989. Abbreviated NAB.

19. A[rno] C. Gaebelein, *The Prophet Daniel* (Grand Rapids, Michigan: Kregel Publications, 1955), 77.

20. Walter M. Abbott, *The Documents of Vatican II* (New York: Herder and Herder, 1966). Quoted by V. Norskov Olsen, *Papal Supremacy, the Roman Catholic Cornerstone and Stumblingblock, and American Democracy, Its Religious Roots and Heritage* (Loma Linda/Riverside, California: Loma Linda University Press, 1987), 140, 141.

21. See pp. 685-698.

22. Ellen G. White, *The Great Controversy Between Christ and Satan* (Nampa, Idaho: Pacific Press Publishing Association, 1911), 588.

23. Ellen G. White, *Testimonies for the Church,* (Nampa, Idaho: Pacific Press Publishing Association, 1948) 7:182.

24. Ellen G. White, *Signs of the Times,* Nov. 1, 1899.

25. Ellen G. White, *The Spirit of Prophecy* (Nampa, Idaho: Pacific Press Publishing Association, 1884), 4:277, 278.

26. White, *The Great Controversy,* 561, 562. See also White, *Testimonies,* 7:182. A full discussion concerning the revival of papal power is beyond the scope of this study. If you wish to pursue this subject in depth, see *The Shape of the Coming Crisis,* by this author (Nampa, Idaho: Pacific Press Publishing Association, 1998), 58-82.

CHAPTER FOUR

Antiochus Epiphanes and Daniel Eight

For the greater part of two thousand years most students of Bible prophecy agreed that the visions of Daniel 2 and 7 are parallel prophecies, each of which outlines the same succession of empires, but from different perspectives. Daniel 2 portrays these empires with emphasis on a political viewpoint, Daniel 7 with emphasis on a religio-political point of view. Most of these Bible students also agreed that, besides simply recapitulating the sequence of empires in chapter 2, Daniel 7 introduces a new power—the little horn—and elaborates on events to occur during its existence—which occupies the time of the feet of iron and clay of chapter 2.

What is true of Daniel 7 with respect to Daniel 2 is also true of Daniel 8 with respect to Daniel 2 and 7. The prophecy of Daniel 8 recapitulates the sequence of empires of the earlier chapters, omitting Babylon, which was passé by the time it was written, but expanding further on the nature and activities of the little horn. And this prophecy offers a third perspective, that of the sanctuary.

As pointed out in chapter 2, since about 1830 there has been a shift by conservative Protestants away from the historicist interpretation of Daniel 8. This shift, as will be shown, has resulted in unwarranted interpretations of Bible prophecy.

Futurists, who interpret the little horn of the male goat to be an Anti-christ-yet-to-come, postulate a gap of some two thousand years from Christ's ascension to Antichrist's appearance just before the Second Coming. Preterists, on the other hand, interpret the little horn to be Antiochus IV—also called Antiochus Epiphanes (who ruled 175-163 B.C.). In so doing they undermine Daniel's credibility as a prophet inspired by God, making his prediction a *vaticinium ex eventu*—a "prophecy" after the event, and they open an unjustifiable gap of more than two thousand years during which Daniel's prophecies offer no guidance to the people of God.

The futurist gap is unwarranted because there is *not a scintilla of biblical evidence* justifying a hiatus of some two thousand years between the 69th and 70th weeks of Daniel 9. This interpretation was an invention devised by the papacy to deflect the accusing finger of prophecy from itself, as we have seen. Why should God give such detailed information with respect to the Babylonian, Medo-Persian, Grecian, and Roman Empires in Daniel 2, 7, and 8 and then provide no information for His people regarding the next two millenniums?

As for the preterist theory that the little horn represents the Seleucid king Antiochus Epiphanes and that the 1,260 days began and ended during his reign, this chapter will show that this theory has no foundation.

But this isn't all. The truth is that, even on their own terms, futurism and preterism do not satisfy the specifications of the prophecy of the little horn in Daniel 7 or of the little horn of Daniel 8, while historicism does.

As pointed out above, Daniel 8 covers the same ground as chapters 2 and 7 (Babylon, nearing the end of its career, being passed over), *but from the point of view of the overthrow and restoration of God's sanctuary.* Chapter 9, then, after a lengthy prayer, explains the time factor not completely dealt with in chapter 8. (For the reader's convenience, chapters 8 and 9 of Daniel as translated in *Young's Literal Translation of the Holy Bible* have been printed in the appendix to this book.*)

---

* We have chosen Young's translation because in general it is less interpretative than most translations and usually italicizes supplied words, which most translations do not do.

OPEN SECRETS OF THE ANTICHRIST

The ram and the male goat

In Daniel 8:20, 21, the angel declares in plain Hebrew that the ram represents "the kings of Media and Persia" and the male goat, "the king of Javan"—the name by which the Jews referred to Greece. In fact, the New King James Version (NKJV) renders this phrase "the kingdom of Greece."[1] The translation "kingdom" rather than "king" is interpretative, but, as will now be shown, it makes good sense.

If the he-goat stands for "the *king* of Greece" (RSV, NIV, etc.), saying that the large horn between its eyes represents the "first king" of Greece is tautological nonsense. However, if, in harmony with the principle established in chapter 1 that a horn in Daniel and Revelation stands for a *succession* of kings (a kingdom with its dynasty or dynasties), not a single king, and the goat represents the *kingdom* of Greece, then the large horn, which was broken off, logically would stand for Alexander the Great *and his successors.*

Did Alexander have a dynastic succession? *He did!* Many interpreters of Daniel 8 miss this point. Similarly, many exegetes overlook the fact that the Greek Empire did not break up immediately into four kingdoms upon Alexander's death. A period of more than twenty years elapsed between Alexander's death and the emergence of the four kingdoms represented by the four horns, and during this interval *Alexander had successors.* Here is what happened.

When Alexander died in 323 B.C., his army vested power jointly between his illegitimate half brother, Arrhidaeus, and Alexander's unborn son by Roxana, a Persian princess. These two rulers became known, respectively, as Philip III and Alexander IV[2]—the latter of whom was also known as Alexander Aegeus (literally and perhaps significantly, "Alexander the Goat"). So Alexander did have successors, even if we disregard the fact that some of his leading generals eventually claimed to be his successor. In addition, we should note that during the two decades that followed Alexander's death, several of those generals each tried to unite the empire under one head—himself. However, as the fourth century neared its close, *all pretenses of accomplishing this objec-*

46

tive were dropped. This is an important point. *The New Encyclopedia Britannica* confirms this fact in a most striking way. It says:

> The year 306 was marked by a spate of kingship claims. After Demetrius' seizure of Cyprus, Antigonus [Monophthalmus ("the one-eyed")] assumed the title of king for himself and his son—a clear implication that they were kings of Alexander's empire. A year later Ptolemy also took the title. . . . Cassander, Lysimachus, and Seleucus quickly followed suit. . . .
>
> Antigonus' enemies now prepared seriously to oppose him. A new coalition of Cassander, Lysimachus, Ptolemy, and Seleucus . . . made ready to confront [Antigonus] Monophthalmus, who recalled Demetrius from Athens. Father and son met the combined forces of Lysimachus and Seleucus . . . at Ipsus in Phrygia (301). Antigonus lost the battle, perishing in the melee; Demetrius escaped.
>
> The victors shared the spoils. Lysimachus took Asia Minor to the Taurus (except parts of Lycia and Pisidia, which became Ptolemaic, and Cilicia, which was governed for a time by Cassander's brother Pleistarchus). Seleucus declared his claim to Syria, but he did not care to press it against his benefactor, Ptolemy, who held all south of Aradus and Damascus. Cassander remained satisfied with his European possessions. *The battle of Ipsus marked the end of all pretenses that the empire would be united.*[3]

This fourfold division of the Grecian Empire lasted only a little more than a decade (301-288 B.C.). But, in harmony with the principle that a horn represents a kingdom *with its succession of rulers,* each of the four kingdoms that divided up Alexander's empire had its dynasties— *even Cassander's short-lived kingdom.* (Cassander was succeeded by his son, Alexander, then by Demetrius, son of Antigonus.)

In 288 B.C., Lysimachus defeated Demetrius and added Greece and Macedonia to his kingdom. In this way the first of the four horns disappeared. For the next hundred and twenty years, the "empire" consisted of three divisions. Then, in 168 B.C., Rome defeated the Graeco-Macedonian segment of the empire at the Battle of Pydna, leaving only two divisions. Daniel 11 mentions these two divisions—the Seleucid and Ptolemaic kingdoms—calling them, respectively, the king of the north and the king of the south.

Daniel refers to the divided Greek Empire as "their kingdom" (Dan. 8:23), that is, the "empire" of Alexander's warring generals. In this connection the prophecy says that "in the *latter time* of their kingdom" (v. 23, NKJV*)*, that is, when the divided Grecian Empire was coming to its end, a sixth horn, *a new kingdom with its succession of rulers,* would arise, literally, "from littleness" (v. 9, Amplified[4]). This "king"—or as we have seen, kingdom with its dynasty of kings—is described as being "fierce of face, and understanding hidden things" (Dan. 8:23, Young), or, as the NKJV renders it, "having fierce features, who understands sinister schemes." This sixth horn is usually termed the "little horn of Daniel 8."

Problems with the Antiochus Epiphanes view

As mentioned earlier in this chapter, many modern exegetes, both Protestant and Catholic, interpret this horn to be Antiochus Epiphanes. However, there are serious objections to this interpretation. Sir Isaac Newton, the great scientist, mathematician, and student of Bible prophecy, pointed out some of these objections:

> This last horn is by some taken for ANTIOCHUS EPIPHANES, but not very judiciously. A horn of a Beast is never taken for a single person: it always signifies a new kingdom, and the kingdom of ANTIOCHUS was an old one. ANTIOCHUS reigned over one of the four horns, and the little horn was a fifth* under its proper kings. This horn was at first a little one, and

---

*Newton says the little horn was a fifth horn because he is considering only the dynasties of the four horns and thus excludes the Alexandrian dynasty symbolized by the great horn.

waxed exceeding great, but so did not ANTIOCHUS. It is described [as] great above all the former horns, and so was not ANTIOCHUS. His kingdom on the contrary was weak, and tributary to the ROMANS, and he did not enlarge it. The horn was a King of fierce countenance, and destroyed wonderfully, and prospered and practised; that is, he prospered in his practices against the holy people: but ANTIOCHUS was frightened out of EGYPT by a mere message of the ROMANS, and afterwards routed and baffled by the JEWS. The horn was mighty by another's power, ANTIOCHUS acted by his own. The horn stood up against the Prince of the Host of heaven, the Prince of Princes; and this is the character not of ANTIOCHUS but of ANTI-CHRIST. The horn cast down the Sanctuary to the ground, and so did not ANTIOCHUS; he left it standing. The Sanctuary and Host were trampled underfoot 2300 days; and in DANIEL'S Prophecies days are put for years: but the profanation of the Temple in the reign of ANTIOCHUS did not last for so many natural days. These [prophetic days] were to last till the time of the end.[5]

Those who believe that the horn that came from "littleness" represents Antiochus Epiphanes try to interpret the "evening-morning 2,300"* of Daniel 8:14 to be 1,150 days (e.g., GNB). This interpretation *assumes* that the "evening-morning 2,300" is derived from 1,150 evening sacrifices plus 1,150 morning sacrifices.[†] However, as will now be shown, this interpretation misses an important point and therefore must be rejected.

In the first place, these daily sacrifices are never called the "evening and morning sacrifice" or "burnt offering," but always "morning and evening sacrifice" or "burnt offering." This transposition may seem inconsequential, but it is definitive: *evening followed by morning is the*

---

*Young's Literal Translation of the Holy Bible reads: "And he saith unto me, Till evening-morning two thousand and three hundred, then is the holy place declared right."

† The following texts use the expression "morning and evening sacrifices": 2 Chron. 13:11; 31:3; cp. 2:4; Ezra 3:3; Num. 28:4.

biblical way of referring to a twenty-four hour day (see Gen. 1:5, 8, 13, 19, 23, 31). Not only that, but it was also this consideration that justified the translation "evening and morning, two thousand and three hundred days"[6] in the Septuagint version[*] of the Old Testament.

Carl F. Keil, editor of the widely used Keil and Delitzsch *Biblical Commentary on the Old Testament*, laid to rest the argument in favor of 1,150 days (in other words, that "evening-morning 2,300" means 1,150 whole days) by saying:

> When the Hebrews wish to express separately day and night, the component parts of a day of a week, then the number of both is expressed. They say, e.g., forty days and forty nights (Gen. vii:4, 12; Ex xxiv:18; 1 Kings xix:8), and three days and three nights (Jonah i:17; Matt xii:40), but not eighty or six days-and-nights, when they wish to speak of forty or three full days. *A Hebrew reader could not possibly understand the period of time 2300 evening-mornings of 2300 half days or 1150 whole days,* because evening and morning at the creation constituted not the half but the whole day. . . . We must therefore take the words as they are, i.e., understand them of 2300 whole days.[7]

In the second place, 1 Maccabees—the primary source of information for this period of Jewish history—gives precise dates for the suspension and resumption of the temple sacrifices in the time of Antiochus Epiphanes. While the author of 1 Maccabees believed Antiochus Epiphanes to be the fulfillment of Daniel 8's little horn prophecy, *the dates he gave for Antiochus's desecration of the temple can in no way be reconciled with either 2,300 evening-mornings or 1,150 days.* First Maccabees 1:54 says that Antiochus interrupted the temple services beginning on the 15th of Kislev in the year 145 of the Seleucid era,[8] or

---

[*] See also D-R, Knox, CLB, etc.

168 B.C.,* and 1 Maccabees 4:52 states that the services were resumed on the 25th of Kislev in the 148th year of the Seleucid era, or 165.† This is a period of three years and ten days, which is at least 60 days short of the 1,150 days posited by those who interpret the prophecy in that way.‡ Conversely, if the evening-mornings equal 2,300 days, it is 1,210 days too long to fit Antiochus's incursion.§

Concerning the futility of trying to make the 2,300 evening-mornings fit the times of Antiochus Epiphanes, Charles H. H. Wright, the Irish Hebraist, theologian, and philologist, rightly said, "All efforts . . . to harmonize the period, whether expounded as 2,300 days or as 1,150 days, with any precise historical epoch mentioned in the Books of the Maccabees or in Josephus have proved futile."[9]

Faced with this dilemma, Canon Frederic W. Farrar (an advocate of the Antiochus Epiphanes interpretation) conceded that, when it comes to the 2,300 evening-mornings, "no minute certainty about the exact dates is attainable."[10] And Herbert C. Leupold, professor of Old Testament exegesis at Capital University, Columbus, Ohio, put this difficulty even more pungently:

> Reckon as you will, there is no clear-cut period of either the one or the other length. Then the *juggling of facts and figures begins.* . . .
> There is something basically wrong with such computations.[11]

Indeed, there *is* something wrong! Prophetic expositors who try to apply the little horn of Daniel 8 to Antiochus Epiphanes either ignore or fudge the facts and figures.

Those who interpret the little horn to be Antiochus Epiphanes make another mistake: they *assume* it grew out of one of the four preceding horns. But the Hebrew text does not support this assumption.

---

* Some authorities say 167.
† Some authorities say 164.
‡ 1,150 - 1,090 = 60. (1,090 comes from 360 x 3 + 10.)
§ 2,300 - 1,090 = 1,210. (1,090 comes from 360 x 3 + 10.)

In Daniel 8:8, 9, the Hebrew noun "horn(s)" is feminine, but the pronoun "them" is masculine. Consequently, "them" *cannot* refer back to "horns" as its antecedent. On the other hand, the word "wind(s)" can be either masculine or feminine and, therefore, "them" *can* refer back to "winds." Accordingly, the little horn came from *one of the four winds,* the Hebrew way of saying, from one of the four cardinal points of the compass[12] without specifying from which direction. However, the direction becomes clear from the context. In order to have moved "toward the south, and toward the east, and toward the pleasant land"— Palestine— (Dan. 8:9), *it must have come from the west,* as will be shown.

On the basis of the foregoing explanation, it is evident that Antiochus Epiphanes does not meet the specifications of the little horn of Daniel 8. What power, then, *does* fulfill these specifications? This question will be taken up in the next chapter.

---

1. *Holy Bible: The New King James Version* (New York: Thomas Nelson Publishers, 1982), Daniel 8:21. Abbreviated NKJV.

2. *The New Encyclopædia Britannica,* "Seleucid Dynasty," (Chicago: Encyclopædia Britannica, Inc., 1985), 20:289.

3. Ibid., 290, 291. Emphasis supplied.

4. *The Amplified Bible* (Grand Rapids, Mich.: Zondervan Bible Publishers, 1965).

5. *Sir Isaac Newton's Daniel and the Apocalypse,* Sir William Whitla, ed. (London: John Murray, 1922), 222. Quoted by Maxwell in *God Cares,* 1:192. The capitals are Newton's.

6. *The Septuagint Bible: The Oldest Version of the Old Testament,* Charles Thomson, trans.; C. A. Muses, rev. ed. (Indian Hills, Colorado: The Falcon's Wing Press, 1954), Daniel 8:14.

7. C. F. Keil and F. Delitzsch, *Biblical Commentary on the Old Testament,* M.G. Easton, trans. (Grand Rapids, Mich.: Wm. B. Eerdmans Publishing Co., 1959), 25:303, 304. Quoted by Maxwell in *God Cares,* 1:180. Emphasis his.

8. New Oxford Annotated RSV, p. [223], Apocrypha section.

9. Charles H. H. Wright, *Daniel and His Prophecies* (London: Williams and Norgate, 1906), 186, 187. Quoted by Gerhard F. Hasel, "The 'Little Horn,' the Saints, and the Sanctuary in Daniel 8," *The Sanctuary and the Atonement,* Arnold V. Wallenkampf and W. Richard Lesher, eds. (Washington, D.C.: Review and Herald Publishing Association, 1981), 220, note 149. Abbreviated *The Sanctuary.*

10. F. W. Farrar, *The Book of Daniel; The Expositor's Bible,* W. Robertson Nicoll, ed. (New York: A. C. Armstrong and Son, 1895), 266.

11. C. H. Leupold, *Exposition of Daniel* (Grand Rapids: Baker Book House, 1975), 355, 356. Quoted by Desmond Ford in דניאל *(Daniel)* (Nashville, Tennessee: Southern Publishing Association, 1978), 173. Emphasis supplied.

12. Hasel, op. cit., 182, 183.

CHAPTER FIVE

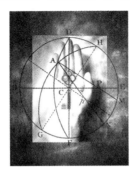

Rome, the Horn That Came From "Littleness"

A careful analysis and comparison of the histories of Antiochus IV (Epiphanes) and Rome in the light of the prophecy of Daniel 8 shows that Rome fulfills the specifications of the little horn, while Antiochus does not. Several problems with respect to the Antiochus interpretation have already been pointed out. In this chapter we will look at some additional problems, and we will couple them with evidence showing that Rome fulfills the specifications with striking exactness.

When the Roman Republic became a power to be reckoned with in the eastern Mediterranean, it was a new "horn"—*a new nation with its own succession of rulers.* By contrast, the Seleucid kingdom was an old horn—and Antiochus Epiphanes constituted an integral part of that old Seleucid dynasty.

In harmony with the prediction that the sixth horn would come forth, literally, "from littleness,"[1] the Latins (the original Romans) were comparatively few in number when they began to rise to prominence. This was not true of Antiochus, who inherited the largest and probably most populous segment of Alexander's empire.

The prophecy declares that the little horn would become "mighty, but not by . . . [its] own power" (v. 24, NKJV). In harmony with this specification, the early Romans owed their political and military power to the alliances they formed with their neighbors and other nations. This was not true of Antiochus. He had few allies and had to depend on his own resources for his strength.

The prophecy goes on to say that the little horn would become "exceedingly great" (v. 9, see RSV, NEB, NASB) as the "kingdom," or empire, of the four Greek horns came to its "latter end" (Dan. 8:23). Since the divided Greek kingdom (which consisted first of four parts, then of three, and finally two) lasted from 301 to 30 B.C., the latter part of this period came after 168 B.C., when Rome was becoming a power to be reckoned with in the eastern Mediterranean. Not so with Antiochus. He ruled mostly just before the middle of this period (175 to 164). But more importantly, it cannot be said that either he or his kingdom became "great"—let alone *exceedingly great.* His father, Antiochus III, also called "Antiochus the Great," was greater than he was.

An incident that occurred when Antiochus moved against Egypt in 168 B.C. (briefly mentioned by Sir Isaac Newton as noted in the last chapter) establishes beyond reasonable doubt that it was Rome, not Antiochus or his kingdom, that was becoming exceedingly great. As a young man, Antiochus "lived fourteen impressionable years [as a hostage] in Rome."[2] While there, he came to know only too well Rome's military strength. Years later, after he ascended the throne of the Seleucid Empire, he was successful in waging war against Egypt. However, he had hardly savored victory when an envoy from the Roman Senate, Caius Popilius Leanas, confronted him with an ultimatum demanding his immediate withdrawal. When Antiochus demurred, Leanas drew the famous circle around him in the sand and demanded an answer before Antiochus stepped out of it. Faced with Rome's superior strength and his relative weakness, Antiochus was forced to yield to Rome's demand and withdraw his forces from Egypt.[3]

On his return from his war with Egypt, Antiochus passed through Palestine and took out his frustration on the hapless Jews. But even in this enterprise he was not ultimately successful. In time, the Jews, under the leadership of the Maccabees—and *with Rome's backing, be it noted*—harried his armies out of the "Glorious Land."[4]

Rome's movements fulfill prophecy

Daniel 8:9 describes the expansion of the sixth or little horn. It says that this power moved "toward the south, toward the east, and toward the Glorious Land" (NKJV). Did Rome fulfill this specification of the prophecy? *It did!* In 190 B.C., when friction broke out between Antiochus III and Rome, Egypt (situated southward from Rome) sided with the latter against the Seleucid kingdom. Thus, Egypt came under the political influence of Rome. *The Roman horn had moved southward.*

In the war that followed, the Seleucid kingdom (situated eastward from Rome) was defeated at the battle of Magnesia, and two years later (188) Antiochus III became a Roman tributary. (It was after this war, incidentally, that Antiochus IV [Epiphanes] was sent to Rome as a hostage.) *Rome had moved eastward.*

Twenty years later (168), when Rome backed the Jews (inhabitants of the "Glorious Land") against Antiochus Epiphanes, *Rome moved toward Judea,* the Glorious Land. The alliance that the Jews and Romans formed eventually led to Roman domination of Judea.

How do the movements of Antiochus Epiphanes square with the specifications of Daniel's prophecy? *Not well at all.* True, he first marched south and attacked Egypt (168), on the way passing through the Glorious Land. But then, instead of moving eastward, he attacked the Glorious Land. It was only *after* this that Antiochus moved eastward, eventually dying in Babylon. So Antiochus failed to fulfill the sequence specified by the prophecy.

Daniel's prophecy predicted that the little horn would "cast down" "the place of . . . [the] sanctuary" of the "Prince of the host" (Dan. 8:11, NKJV). Did Antiochus do this? No. He reigned over a century and a half *before* the Prince of the host, Jesus Christ, was born. Moreover, although Antiochus interrupted the Jewish temple services for three years and ten days, as we have seen, he did not destroy the temple as it was prophesied the little horn would do.

Did Rome fulfill these specifications? *It did!* Rome stood up against Christ, "the Prince of princes," through its procurator, Pontius Pilate, who condemned Him to be crucified. And the Romans did destroy the temple in Jerusalem in A.D. 70 as a consequence of "the people of the prince who is to come" (Dan. 9:26, NKJV)—in other words, the Jews—rejecting their Messiah.

Rome's policy of ruthlessly suppressing any individual or nation that refused to kowtow to it fulfills the prediction that the little horn would "destroy fearfully, and . . . prosper and thrive" (Dan. 8:24). In its oppression, pagan Rome "grew up to the host of heaven; and it cast down *some* of the host and *some* of the stars to the ground, and trampled them" (v. 10, NKJV). Verse 24 interprets the "host" to be God's "mighty and *also* holy people" (NKJV).

During the early centuries of the Christian era, Rome frequently put to death both Christians and Jews, both of whom professed to be God's people, and seemingly prospered in this ruthless policy (v. 24).[5]

Further Roman fulfillments

In chapter 3, it was shown that the fourth beast of Daniel 7 and its little horn represent pagan and papal Rome as *separate* entities—the beast representing pagan Rome; the little horn, papal Rome. By contrast the little horn of Daniel 8 *combines* the pagan and papal aspects of Rome under a single symbol, and yet, as will be shown, both powers remain distinct one from the other.

In this connection Gerhard F. Hasel, late dean of the Seventh-day Adventist Theological Seminary, noted that "there is an important change in syntax between Daniel 8:9-10 and 8:11-12,"[6] and made the following significant point:

> The verbal forms in Dan 8:9-10 are feminine with but one exception in the first clause of v 9 which is easily explained on the basis of the lack of concord [agreement] of subject and verb when the verb

precedes the subject and the subject is inanimate or animal. . . . All other verbs in vs 9-10 are feminine, depending on the gender of "horn" [feminine]. In vs 11-12 we are confronted with a new situation. The gender of all Hebrew verbs in these verses is masculine.[7]

On the basis of these facts Hasel concluded that "this shift in gender . . . indicates on the one hand that the metaphor 'horn' is dropped and that the reality or power for which the horn stands [in other words, papal Rome] is in view."[8]

To put it simply, "the gender shift [in these verses] points to a change [from pagan Rome] to Rome in its sole papal phases."[9]

The fact that there is a change in gender, suggesting two entities, while there is but *one* horn, leads to the conclusion that while the prophecy distinguishes between pagan and papal Rome, yet it also recognizes a continuity from one to the other. In other words, while papal Rome (a religious organization) is distinct from pagan Rome (a secular organization), yet papal Rome grew out of pagan Rome and reflects many of its characteristics—and by its own admissions, as we have seen, claims to have taken the place of pagan Rome.

The very fact that the Catholic Church calls itself "Roman" and that the papal "see," or headquarters of that church, is situated in the ancient capital of the Roman Empire, suggests a connection and at the same time a distinction between the Roman Empire and the Roman Church.

Harry A. Dawe, the author of a modern history textbook, describes the relationship between pagan and papal Rome in these words:

> In the West, the Church took over the defense of Roman civilization. The emperor gave up the [pagan] title of Pontifex Maximus (high priest) because the Roman gods were no longer worshipped. The bishop of Rome assumed these priestly functions, and this is why the Pope today is sometimes referred to as the Pontiff. When the Huns . . . threatened to take and destroy the city of Rome [A.D. 452], it was the leader of the Christian Church, Pope

Leo [I], not the emperor, who met the barbarian. Attila was so impressed with the Pope's spiritual power that he turned back. What Leo said to Attila remains unknown, but what is significant is the fact that it was the Pope and not the emperor who stood at the gates of Rome. *The Roman Empire had become the Christian Church.*[10]

If the foregoing is true, it follows that the first part of the prophecy (Dan. 8:9, 10) applies to pagan Rome and the second part (vs. 11, 12) to papal Rome. It therefore follows that, in the elaboration of verses 9, 10 in verses 23, 24, pagan Rome is brought to view, whereas verse 25, elaborating on verses 11, 12, refers to papal Rome. And yet, in some respects, as we have seen, the prophecy applies to both powers.

Both pagan and papal Rome

The prophecy states that the little horn would exalt itself "as high as the Prince of the host; and by him [the little horn] the daily *sacrifices** were taken away, and the place of His sanctuary was cast down" (Dan. 8:11, NKJV). In a sense, pagan Rome exalted itself as high as the Prince of the host when, through its procurator, Pontius Pilate, it condemned Christ to death by crucifixion. But in a more important sense, the papal authorities' claim that the Roman pontiff "is of so great dignity and power that he forms one and the same tribunal with Christ"[11] exalts the pope to a position as high as the "Prince of the host," Jesus Christ.

While pagan Rome literally cast down the temple in Jerusalem in A.D. 70, the more important casting down was the one carried on during the 1,260 years of papal dominance. It was during those centuries that the papacy, figuratively speaking, "cast down" to this earth "the place of . . . [Christ's] sanctuary" in heaven by substituting the oft-repeated sacrifice of the Mass for Christ's once-for-all sacrifice on Calvary (see Heb. 7:26, 27; 9:26).

This two-phase casting down and substitution is called the setting up of "the abomination that makes desolate" (Dan. 11:31; 12:11, RSV).

---

* In the NKJV, italics indicate a supplied word rather than emphasis.

In the prophecy recorded in Matthew 24, Christ spoke about the first part of this two-phase casting down. He called it "the abomination of desolation" (24:15-18, NKJV)—referring, by this term, to the destruction of the temple in A.D. 70. Daniel 8:11 speaks of both phases of this casting down by the abomination of desolation. The first phase was Imperial Rome's destruction of the temple in A.D. 70; the second phase, the casting down of the heavenly sanctuary by ecclesiastical Rome during the 1,260 years of papal dominance.

The last clause of Daniel 8:25 (NKJV) predicts that the little horn would "be broken without *human* hand." During the fourth and fifth centuries A.D., pagan Rome *was* broken by human hands—the hands of the barbarian kingdoms that parceled out the Roman Empire. As a result, that portion of the prophecy cannot apply to pagan Rome. It must apply to papal Rome alone—for according to the prophecy, the little horn will be broken by God's superhuman hand when He sets up His eternal kingdom at the second coming of Christ.

So, Rome, both pagan and papal, not Antiochus Epiphanes, offers the most satisfactory interpretation of the character and activity of the little horn of Daniel 8.

---

1. Dan. 8:9, Amplified; cp. *Strong's Exhaustive Concordance.*

2. Will Durant, *The Story of Civilization: The Life of Greece* (New York: Simon and Schuster, 1966), 2:574.

3. Roy A. Stewart, "Maccabees," *The International Standard Bible Encyclopedia,* rev. ed., Geoffrey W. Bromiley, gen. ed. (Grand Rapids, Mich.: William B. Eerdmans Publishing Company, 1986), 3:198.

4. *A History of the Jewish People*, H. H. Ben-Sasson, ed. (Cambridge, Massachusetts: Harvard University Press, 1976), 207.

5. *The Works of Josephus,* William Whiston, trans. (Halifax: Milner and Sowerby, 1860), Bk. VI, chap. iii, par. 4, pp. 602, 603.

6. *The Sanctuary,* 188.

7. Ibid.

8. Ibid.

9. Ibid.

10. Harry A. Dawe, *Ancient Greece and Rome,* World Cultures in Perspective (Columbus, Ohio: Charles E. Merrill Publishing Co., 1970), 188. Quoted by Maxwell in *God Cares,* 1:160. Emphasis supplied.

11. Ferraris, *op. cit.,* 29. Quoted in *Bible Students' Source Book,* 680.

CHAPTER SIX

"Until When Is the Vision to Be?"

The climax of the vision of Daniel 8, and in fact the pivotal point of the entire book, is the question and answer in verses 13 and 14. A literal rendering of the question reads: " 'Until when [is] the vision [to be]—[about] the continual [mediation] and the transgression causing horror, to make both sanctuary and host a trampling?' "[1] And a literal reading of the answer is: " 'Till evening-morning two thousand three hundred, then is the holy place [or sanctuary] declared right' " (Young).

William H. Shea, former associate director of the Biblical Research Institute in Silver Spring, Maryland, elaborates on the significance of this interpretation. He says:

> All that precedes this inquiry must be included in the reference to this (single) vision. Thus the 2300-day period must include both the prophecies about the Persian ram and the Grecian he-goat as well as the description of the actions of the little horn. If this were not the case, then the inquiring holy one should have distinguished between two preceding visions, which he did

not do. In other words, the holy one did not inquire how long would the little horn take away the *tamid,* etc.[2]

So, the question asked is not, "How long [shall be] the vision?" as most translators render it, but, "Until when [is] the vision [to be]?" The significance of this translation is, as Hasel points out, that "the question 'until when' [unlike the question 'how long'] *has its focus on the point of termination* of the time period indicated."[3]

Yet, as Hasel goes on to explain:

> When the point of termination is stressed the inevitable matter of the beginning of the time period comes into view also. In other words, the beginning and end belong together and implicitly also what takes place during the vision.[4]

Since the vision begins with the ram, or Media-Persia (Dan. 8:20), which held sway from 539 to 331 B.C., the "evening-morning two thousand three hundred" vision must begin during the time of the Medo-Persian Empire; in other words, some time between 539-331. But the 2,300 evening-mornings do not end during the Medo-Persian period, they continue until "the time of the end" (v. 17); in other words, through the Grecian and little-horn periods. So, again, the vision "is not limited [to Antiochus Epiphanes or] to the 'little horn' period alone."[5] It continues "until the time of the end."

Since the 2,300 evening-mornings begin during the Medo-Persian period, continue through Greece and Rome in its two phases, and only end in "the time of the end" (v. 17), Hasel is correct in asserting that it is *"clear beyond the shadow of a doubt that the year-day principle is functioning in Dan[iel] 8."*[6] After all, the rise and fall of just one of the empires depicted in this prophecy covered centuries, not merely 2,300 literal days, much less 1,150 literal days as some contend.

At the time Daniel received the vision of the ram and the he-goat (548/547 B.C.),[7] a little more than a decade remained of the 70 years of captivity Jeremiah had prophesied (see Jer. 29:10; cp. 25:11, 12). This captivity began in 605 B.C. and was due to end in 536 B.C. During the greater part of this time Jerusalem and its temple (or sanctuary) lay in ruins, its ceremonies suspended (Dan. 9:17).

The evidence, therefore, appears conclusive that, having been told that at the end of 2,300 years the sanctuary would be *nisdaq** (variously translated "cleansed," "purified," "emerge victorious," "put in a right condition," "restored to its rightful place," "declared right," etc.), Daniel concluded that the Jewish temple and its services would remain in a desolate condition far beyond the 70 years prophesied by Jeremiah. Hence, the 2,300 days/years would *not* reach their termination until "the time of the end"—many centuries in the future.

The hope of all pious Jews in Daniel's day was that at the end of Jeremiah's 70 years they would be free to return to their homeland, rebuild Jerusalem, and restore the temple's services. So, it is little wonder that Daniel "was astonished by the vision" and that he "fainted and was sick for days" (v. 27, NKJV*)*. What pious Jew wouldn't have reacted in the same way?

Two words for vision: chazon and mareh

The use of two Hebrew words in Daniel 8 and 9 provides a link between these two chapters—specifically, between the 70 weeks of years prophecy in chapter 9 and the 2,300 days/years prophecy of chapter 8:14. This link is important, because without it we would have no starting point for the 2,300 years.

The two Hebrew words are *chazon* and *mareh.* While both terms can—and are—translated "vision," they are not exactly synonymous. *Chazon* means "a vision in the ecstatic [i.e., prophetic] state."[8] This word is used to refer to the whole vision of chapter 8 (see, e.g., vs. 1, 2,

---

* Different spellings with diacritical markings are often used in transliterating Hebrew words. For simplification, a single spelling of words is used throughout this study and diacritical markings have been omitted. The meaning of *nisdaq* will be discussed in chapter 7.

13, 15, 17, 26b). *Mareh,* on the other hand, means a "sight, phenomenon, spectacle, appearance."[9] This word is used of the "appearance"
within the vision of the two beings, one of whom raises the question
"Until when . . . ?" that the other answers with "till evening-morning
two thousand three hundred" (see vs. 16, 26a, 27).

It was the *mareh* that, in verse 16, Gabriel was commissioned to
help Daniel understand. But at the close of chapter 8, Daniel says he
"was astonished by the *mareh*" and did not understand it. Then, in Daniel
9:23, Gabriel appears to the prophet again and tells him to "consider
the word and understand the *mareh*." So, Gabriel's explanation in chapter 9 was given specifically to explain the 2,300 evening-mornings of
chapter 8.

Now let's work in a more detailed way through Daniel 8 and 9:
Gabriel commences to fulfill his commission by explaining in literal or
quasi-literal language the meaning of the various symbols of the "vision" *(chazon),* such as the ram, the he-goat, the great horn, the four
horns, and the "king, fierce of face" (see chap. 8:20-25, Young). In verse
26 Gabriel refers to the matter of the "evening-morning two thousand
three hundred," which he calls the *mareh,* or "appearance." Then, in the
latter part of verse 26, he states that the *chazon,* which, as we have seen
began with the Medo-Persian ram and has its fulfillment "after many
days" (Young; cp. v. 17, "the appointed time of the end").

Daniel says that upon hearing this he "fainted, and was sick for
days" (v. 27), after which he "rose and went about the king's busi-
ness." He says he fainted because he "was astonished by the vision
[the *mareh* concerning the "evening-morning two thousand three hun-
dred]." Obviously, Daniel had concluded that the temple in Jerusalem would be trampled down for 2,300 years—far into the distant
future.

It is Daniel's failure to understand why the sanctuary would be
trampled down for so long that underlies his long prayer recorded in
chapter 9:4-19. This explanation is confirmed by the fact that in his
prayer Daniel repeatedly refers to the desolations of Jerusalem (see vs.

12, 16, 18) and pleads for the Lord to cause His face to shine on His sanctuary "that *is* desolate" (v. 17, Young).

But the expression that clinches this conclusion is the prophet's plea *"do not delay,* for Thine own sake, O my God, for Thy name is called on Thy city, and on Thy people" (v. 19, Young; emphasis supplied). Why would Daniel implore God to not delay if he were not concerned that the desolation of the sanctuary had been extended far beyond the 70 years of Jeremiah's prophecy?

But these are not the only links between Daniel 8 and 9.

The 70 weeks and the 2,300 years

Daniel 8 ends with the statement that Daniel didn't understand the *mareh* of the 2,300 evening-mornings.

Now, in response to Daniel's prayer recorded in chapter 9, Gabriel, who had begun to explain that which Daniel did not understand (the 2,300 evening-mornings), returned to continue his explanation. So, Gabriel is a link between the two chapters.

But there is an even stronger link between these chapters, likewise based on various forms of the word *understand.* In Daniel 9:22 Gabriel says he came to give Daniel "understanding," and in verse 23 he explicitly urges the prophet, "Understand thou concerning *the matter* and consider the vision *[mareh]*" that perplexed the prophet, namely, the 2,300 evening-mornings. This must be what he meant since there is no other vision (*chazon*—or *mareh,* for that matter) between Daniel 8 and this verse to which the angel could possibly have been referring. Gabriel then began his explanation of the 2,300 evening-mornings by referring to a time period—which is another link.

A literal translation of Gabriel's first words reads, "Seventy sevens (*shabuim*) . . ." *Shabuim* is a masculine plural noun. As a singular it can mean a period of seven consecutive days; that is, a week. But it can also stand for *seven consecutive years*—for example, " 'You shall count seven sabbaths of years' " (Lev. 25:8, NKJV). The pseudepigraphal

Book of Jubilees and the Mishna also use "week" to mean a heptad of years.

Here's another point: The 2,300 evening-mornings were to reach to "the time of the end" (Dan. 8:17, 26), so the 2,300 evening-mornings must stand for 2,300 years. Therefore, the 70 weeks *must* be weeks of years, not literal weeks. If this were not the case, Gabriel would be "mixing apples and oranges," and his explanation would be no explanation at all.

In support of this conclusion, numerous versions and translations read "seventy weeks of years." (See for example the RSV, TEV, Amplified, Moffatt, CLB, S-G, etc.) These translations also draw on the ancient Septuagint version of the Old Testament for this interpretation. Interestingly, *even a footnote on Daniel 9:24 in the Jewish Tanakh translation interprets these seventy weeks to be "weeks" "of years."* [10]

But the clincher for this interpretation of *shabuim* is found in the fact that, when Daniel wishes to speak of literal weeks, he speaks of "weeks of days" (see Dan. 10:2, 3, Young.) Hence, there is every reason to conclude that in Daniel 9:24-27 the angel was speaking of weeks of years. Thus, Msgr. Knox is absolutely correct, when he insists that the 70 weeks are 70 weeks of years, not weeks of days.*

The beginning of the 70 weeks

The seventy sevens, that is, the seventy weeks-of-years, of Daniel 9 were to begin from the " 'going forth of the word to restore and to build Jerusalem,' " and the first sixty-nine-weeks were to reach "till Messiah the Leader," or "Prince." In other words, according to Daniel 9:25, sixty-nine weeks—that is 483 years—would elapse between the decree to restore and build Jerusalem until Messiah appeared. When did such a word go forth, and hence, when did the 483-year period begin?

---

* See above, pp. 32, 33.

Chronologists generally agree that the maximum limits of Christ's earthly life extended from as early as 7 B.C. to as late as A.D. 33. Backing up 70 *shabuim*—490 years—from the minimal beginning date—7 B.C.—to the beginning of these outer limits, brings us to 497 B.C.* And backing up 490 years from the maximal ending date—A.D. 33, brings us to 456 B.C.† So, if the prophecy is to fit the facts, the decree to restore and rebuild Jerusalem must have been issued between 497 and 456 B.C.

Did someone issue a decree regarding Jerusalem between 497 and 456 B.C.? *Yes!* Ezra 7 says that Artaxerxes I, king of Persia, who reigned from 465 to 423 B.C., issued a decree in his "seventh year" (see Ezra 7:8.) For many years chronologists were uncertain as to whether this decree went into effect in 458 or in 457, but recent studies have settled this point conclusively. Recently, an authority on the subject wrote:

> These documents [the Elephantine papyri], taken together with the Biblical statements of Nehemiah and Ezra, lead to the *inescapable conclusion* that the decree of Artaxerxes I went into effect after Ezra's return from Babylon, in the late summer or early fall of 457 B.C.[11]

The decree Artaxerxes issued in 444 B.C., favored by many Evangelicals[12] by "juggling facts and figures" (Leupold), is speculative and must be rejected.[13] So, the correct date is 457 B.C. This means that the 483 years, or sixty-nine prophetic weeks, begin in 457 B.C. Consequently, they end in the late summer or fall of A.D. 27‡

Just what do the firm dates for the seventy-week prophecy mean for

---

*7 + 490 = 497.

†490 - 33 = 457, but 1 must be subtracted from 457, because we are crossing back from A.D. to B.C., making it 456.

‡483 - 457 = 26, but since there is no zero year between B.C. and A.D. and we are going from B.C. to A.D., 1 year must be added to 26, making it A.D. 27.

the prophecy of the 2,300 days/years? Gabriel began his explanation of the *mareh*, which, as has been shown, has to do with the 2,300 days/ years (cp. Dan. 8:16, 17, 26, 27), by saying that seventy weeks (490 years) are *"chatak"* for Daniel's people. This word *chatak* occurs only once in the Old Testament; translators usually render it, "determined" or "decreed." But this is not the only meaning of *chatak* in Jewish writings. Shea, who has studied the etymology of the word, summarizes his findings by suggesting that *chatak* originally derived from the idea of "cut." He says that this idea still predominates in the word's use in Mishnaic Hebrew even though the Mishna was written a thousand years after Daniel's book.[14]

Shea points out that in 12 out of 14 occurrences of the verb form of *chatak* in the Mishna it means "cutting off" parts of animals in accordance with dietary laws. It is also used to mean to "cut"—that is to trim—a lamp wick, to cut out ore in mining, and to cut off words. *Chatak* is also used in connection with circumcision—cutting off the foreskin. In its substantive form, it is used "at least 18 times to mean 'that which is cut off.' " Only twice is it used with the meaning of "decide" or "determine."[15]

Translating *chatak* as "determined" or "decreed" would make good sense, *if the prophecy had to do only with Daniel's people, the Jews.* But the translation "cut off" makes far better sense if *chatak* refers not only to the period of probation allotted to the Jewish nation, but also to the 2,300 evening-mornings. That was the matter that so perplexed Daniel— and it was the matter that Gabriel began to explain in Daniel 8:16, 27 by saying it pertained to the "time of the end."

Gabriel came expressly to explain the portion of the vision that had to do with the 2,300 evening-mornings. And if the seventy weeks, or 490 years, are to be "cut off," they obviously must be cut off from a longer period of years—2,300 years. Now the question is: How are these years to be cut off?

If the 490 years are cut off from somewhere in the middle of the 2,300 years, Gabriel's "explanation" would shed no light on the beginning or ending of the 2,300 years. But this isn't all: if the 490 years were excised from anywhere except one or the other end of the 2,300 years, they would not be "cut off." In such a case one might say that the 490 years were "cut out from" but not "cut off from."

To be cut off from the 2,300-year period, the 490 years would have to be taken from either the "head"* end or the "tail" end[†] of that longer period. If the 490 years are cut off from the tail end, the tail ends of both periods terminate at the same time. On the other hand, if the 490 years are cut off from the head end, the head ends of both periods *begin* at the same time.

If these two prophetic periods ended simultaneously in A.D. 34 (which has been established as the ending date of the 490-year prophecy), it would mean that the 2,300 years began in 2265 B.C.[‡] But this would be nonsense, for it would mean that the 2,300 evening-mornings, which have to do with "the time of the end," reached its conclusion nearly two millenniums ago. (It would mean, in fact, that most of the period covered by this prophecy occurred before Daniel was born!) In that case it could hardly be called a prophecy—and certainly not a time-of-the-end prophecy.

So, the only part of the 2,300 years that the 490 years can be cut off from and be a prophecy about the time of the end is the "head" end. That means that both the 490 years and the 2,300 years began in the late summer or fall of 457 B.C. *Consequently, the 2,300 years must terminate in the late summer or fall of A.D. 1844, making this prophecy truly a prophecy that concerned the future, the time of the end.*[§]

In 1844 the sanctuary was to be *"nisdaq."* What exactly does *nisdaq* mean? The next chapter will answer this question.

---

*Technically, the *terminus a quo*.

[†] Technically, the *terminus ad quem*.

[‡] 2,300 - 34 = -2266, but 2265 B.C. since there is no zero year.

[§] 2,300 - 457 = 1843, but since there is no 0 year between 1 B.C. and A.D. 1 and we are going *forward* from B.C. to A.D., 1 must be added, making it 1844.

1. See Hasel in *The Sanctuary,* 198; cp. William H. Shea, "The Relationship Between the Prophecies of Daniel 8 and Daniel 9," ibid., 249.

2. Shea, *op. cit.,* 249, 250.

3. Hasel, *op. cit.,* 198. Emphasis supplied.

4. Ibid.

5. Ibid., 199; cp. Shea, ibid., 250.

6. Hasel, ibid. Emphasis supplied.

7. Ibid., 178.

8. Francis Brown, S. R. Driver, and Charles A. Briggs, *The New Brown— Driver—Briggs—Gesenius Hebrew and English Lexicon* (Peabody, Mass.: Hendrickson Publishers, 1979), 909b.

9. Ibid., 302b.

10. *Tanakh: The Holy Scriptures* (New York: The Jewish Publication Society, 1985).

11. Horn and Wood, *op cit.,* 115. Emphasis supplied.

12. Josh McDowell, *The New Evidence That Demands a Verdict* (Nashville: Thomas Nelson Publishers, 1999), 199, 200.

13. For the reason for rejecting 444 B.C., see Gerhard F. Hasel, *The Seventy Weeks, Leviticus, and the Nature of Prophecy* (Washington, D.C.: Biblical Research Institute, 1986), 13-25, 49. Abbreviated *Seventy Weeks.*

14. Shea, ibid., 243.

15. See ibid., 242.

CHAPTER SEVEN

The Cleansing of the Sanctuary and of the Remnant

The 2,300 days/years of Daniel 8 is the longest time prophecy in the Bible. Chapter 6 of this book concludes that the 2,300 years were to end in the late summer or fall of 1844, and chapter 3 says that the 1,260 years of papal ascendancy terminated in late February 1798. Students of prophecy of the historical school have usually designated the period between 1798 and the Second Coming as "the time of the end." They've done so because the vision of the 2,300 evening-mornings (Dan. 8:14) was to terminate *in* or *during* "the time of the end" (v. 26), and, as has been demonstrated, the 2,300 days/years ended in 1844.

In volume 4 of his series *The Prophetic Faith of Our Fathers,* the late LeRoy Froom, who collected the interpretations of literally hundreds of expositors from pre-Christian times down to our day, wrote:

> Following the captivity of Pope Pius VI, in 1798, there was wide recognition on both sides of the Atlantic of the ful-fillment of the close of the fateful 1,260 years. (See Volume

II.) That left only the closing events of Daniel 7 yet to be accomplished—with the awesome judgment scenes at the end of the world.

And now came the remarkable shift of immediate interest and study from Daniel 7 over to Daniel 8 and the 2,300-day prophecy. Among varying interpretations there arose— not only in Britain and Europe, but extending down into Africa and even over into India, and especially here in America—some threescore of earnest students of prophecy, in various denominations and language areas, sounding this new note, *that the 2,300 year-days would end around 1843, 1844, or 1847,* though they differed as to just what would then take place. And a thousand pulpits in Britain alone, we are told, echoed this contention, with scores in North America declaring the same. Never had there been such a chorus since prophetic interpretation began.[1]

In North America the chief proponent of this interpretation was William Miller, a farmer and Baptist lay preacher of Low Hampton, New York. In 1818, after careful Bible study, he concluded, "In about twenty-five years [i.e., c. 1843] . . . all the affairs of our present state [will] be wound up."[2] Miller believed Christ would return to this earth at that time—he thought the earth was the sanctuary of Daniel 8:14— and that Christ would cleanse the earth by putting an end to the present order of things.

Miller began preaching this view in 1831. His message caught the attention of Protestants in North America, and many from various denominations, both leaders and laity, became convinced that his calculations were correct. By 1843 the Advent Movement, or as its critics called it, the Millerite Movement, counted its adherents in the tens of thousands. The Millerites claimed that the message of Christ's imminent return went "to the far corners of the earth through the distribution of their papers to sailors and by the sending of publications to 'every

English and American mission in the world,' 'so far as opportunity . . . offered.' "[3]

In January 1843 Miller set forth his belief that the 2,300 years would end "sometime 'between March 21st 1843, and March 21st 1844.' "[4] Knowing that the Jewish religious year began in the spring, Miller arrived at this conclusion by simply subtracting 457 B.C. (the year Artaxerxes issued his decree) from 2,300 years, apparently forgetting, or perhaps not realizing, that there is no zero year between B.C. and A.D.*

Daniel 12's time periods

In the light of Miller's interpretation, the three time periods of Daniel 12:6-12—the 1,260, the 1,290, and the 1,335 days/years—were significant *because the 1,335 years also were to end in 1843,* as will be shown. Daniel 12:5-12, reads as follows:

> I Daniel looked, and behold, there stood other two [angelic beings], the one on this side, on the bank of the river, and the other on that side, on the bank of the river. And he said to the man clothed in linen, who was above the waters of the river, How long [is it to] the end of these wonders? And I heard the man clothed in linen, who was above the waters of the river; and he held up his right hand and his left hand unto the heavens, and swore by him that liveth for ever that it is for a time, times, and a half; and when the scattering of the power of the holy people shall be accomplished, all these things shall be finished.
>
> And I heard, but I understood not. And I said, My lord, what shall be the end of these things? And he said, Go thy way, Daniel; for these words are closed and sealed till the time of the end. Many shall be purified, and be made white, and be refined; but the wicked shall do wickedly; and none of the wicked

---

* 2,300 - 457 = 1843.

shall understand; but the wise shall understand. And from the time that the continual [sacrifice] is taken away, and the abomination that maketh desolate set up, [there shall be] a thousand, two hundred, and ninety days. Blessed is he that waiteth, and cometh to the thousand three hundred and thirty-five days! But do thou go thy way until the end; and thou shalt rest, and stand in thy lot at the end of the days.[5]

As previously shown, "a time, two times, and half a time" (Dan. 7:25; 12:7, RSV) is the same prophetic time period as the 1,260 days/years. That period began in A.D. 538 and ended in 1798. The 1,290 days/years period is mentioned in close connection with the 1,260 days/years, and the events that were prophesied to take place at the ends of these periods are the same, so they end at the same time. Consequently, Daniel 12:11 should be translated: "From the time of the taking away of the continual [mediation of Christ in the heavenly sanctuary] in order to set up the abomination that makes desolate shall be a thousand two hundred and ninety days."[*] In other words, the little horn's taking away of Christ's continual mediation preceded and prepared the way for its own ascendancy in 538. This means, then, that the beginning point of the 1,290-year prophetic period came thirty years *before* the beginning point of the 1,260-year period. The 1,260 years began with establishment of papal supremacy in A.D. 538; consequently, the 1,290 years began in 508.

As has been shown, 538 was the year the Ostrogoths, the third and *last* of the Arian tribes, was "laid low." Thirty years before this, in 508, the Franks, who subsequently became the French nation, were the *first* Arian tribe to adopt Roman Catholic Christianity. This is

---

[*] Spurrell renders this verse as follows: "Now from the time the daily *sacrifice* shall be removed even to set up the abomination of desolation, *there shall be* a thousand two hundred and ninety days."[6] As in the KJV, italicized words are supplied. Instead of "daily *sacrifice,*" a better translation would be, "continual *mediation.*"

why France has been called the "eldest son of the papacy." It is significant that the Roman Catholic "Byzantine [Eastern Roman] emperor, Anastasius I, . . . conferred upon Clovis [king of the Franks] the honorary title and insignia of consul in 508."[7]

Subsequent to 508, "one after another [of] these barbarian peoples . . . [submitted to the laws of the Church of Rome and counted] it a glory to be the Church's children."[8] By accepting the papal doctrine of the sacrifice of the Mass in place of Christ's "continual" mediation on behalf of sinners in the heavenly sanctuary, the papacy "cast down the place of . . . [Christ's] sanctuary" (Dan. 8:11) and "set up" here on earth "the abomination that maketh desolate" (Dan. 12:11, Darby). The acceptance of this papal doctrine by the Arian tribes prepared the way for the ascendancy of the "little horn" in 538. [3]

The Millerites believed that the 1,335 days/years began at the same time as the 1,290 days/years, that is, in A.D. 508—and hence, that the 1,335 days/years would end in 1843,*—the year William Miller at first believed the 2,300 years would also terminate. Thousands in North America, impressed by Miller's message and calculations, joined the Advent movement, and rejoiced that the ending of the 1,335 days/years in 1843 confirmed Miller's original calculation that the 2,300 days/years would terminate about 1843.

There was great joy among those who believed that Christ would come between the spring equinox of 1843 and the spring equinox of 1844. As Daniel 12:12 says, they felt "blessed." However, when the spring equinox of 1844 passed without Christ's return, they were disappointed, although Miller had always resisted setting a firm date for the end of the 2,300 days. Miller simply encouraged his followers to maintain their faith; the coming of the Lord was near, even at the doors. Even so, enthusiasm in the movement waned from March 21, the spring equinox, to mid-August 1844.

---

*508 + 1,335 = 1843. Note that this prophetic time period does *not* cross from B.C. to A.D., hence, 1843, not 1844.

The Cleansing of the Sanctuary and of the Remnant

The seventh-month movement

Around August 15, 1844, a new expectation inspired the Second Advent believers with renewed hope. After considerable study, Samuel Sheffield Snow, a Congregationalist who had become a Millerite preacher, concluded that the 2,300 days would end on October 22, 1844. He based his conclusion on two grounds: 1) He realized the implications for the mathematics of the 2,300-year prophecy of the fact that there is no zero year between B.C. and A.D.—a fact that the Millerites heretofore had not taken into account. And 2) he noted that the Jewish spring festivals—Passover and the Feast of Weeks (Pentecost)—typified events relating to Christ's first advent, namely His death, resurrection, and Pentecost. He concluded, then, that events related to Christ's second coming must be foreshadowed by the autumn festivals—the Day of Atonement and the Feast of Tabernacles.

By this process of reasoning he came to believe that, as Christ's crucifixion—the antitypical Passover—fell on Passover Day in the spring of A.D. 31, _the antitypical day of atonement would fall on the typical Day of Atonement at the end of the 2,300 years—in other words, in the autumn of 1844._ Snow computed this date to be October 22, 1844, basing his calculations on the calendation, _not_ of the modern Jewish method of calculating the Day of Atonement, but on the older method used by the Kairaite Jews.[9]*

This new, definite date raised the spirit of the Millerites and gave tremendous impetus to the Advent Movement. Those who attended the Exeter, New Hampshire, camp meeting, where Snow first proclaimed this date, left with renewed enthusiasm to announce to the world the imminent coming of Christ.

---

* "With advances in research in ancient astronomy and calendation, we can trace this matter all the way back to its source—the year when Ezra left Babylon. Tracing this trail back that far has indicated that _the Millerites did select the correct date for 10 Tishri by dating it to October 22, 1844._ This point has now been established as definitively as it can be through the study of ancient mathematics and astronomy." William H. Shea, _Selected Studies on Prophetic Interpretation_ (Silver Spring, Md.: General Conference of Seventh-day Adventists, 1982), 137; emphasis supplied.

Aftermath of the Great Disappointment

However, October 22 came and went, and Christ did not return as confidently expected. Many abandoned the Advent movement altogether, and many of those who left it derided those who still believed that God had been in the movement. Some of those who stayed with the movement speculated that the mistake that had been made lay in the calculations and that the end of the 2,300 days was still in the future. These latter Advent believers constituted the major portion of the Millerites. They repeatedly set dates for the Lord's return, only to be repeatedly disappointed.

A smaller group could find no fault with Snow's calculations and believed that something indeed had happened on October 22, 1844. The larger portion of this minority held that Christ had come "spiritually" on that day; these believers became known as "Spiritualizers." A small fragment of those who accepted Snow's calculations, consisting of perhaps as few as fifty individuals, came to understand that the sanctuary Christ was to cleanse at the end of the 2,300 days/years was located, not on earth, but in heaven. They believed that on October 22, 1844, He did indeed begin the work of cleansing the heavenly sanctuary and that when this work has been completed, He would come the second time.[10]

In time these Adventists saw that Christ's work of cleansing the sanctuary involved a work of judgment (Dan. 7:11) and the blotting out of the record of sins confessed and forgiven (see Acts 3:19-21). They believed prophecy predicted the restoration of the biblical "truth" concerning Christ's "continual [mediation]" in the heavenly sanctuary, which the little horn had "cast down . . . to the ground" (Dan. 8:11, 12; cp. 12:11) and replaced with the sacrifice of the Mass and a false sacerdotal system.

Scoffers have ridiculed this new understanding of what happened on October 22, 1844, as "the most colossal, psychological, face-saving phenomenon in religious history."[11] Seventh-day Adventists see it differently. They believe that the evidences of divine approbation that the early Adventists experienced in proclaiming the cleansing of the sanctuary on October 22, 1844, their bitter disappointment the next day, and their new understanding concerning the preaching of the "everlasting gospel" to all the world in the context of a pre-Advent "judgment" (Rev. 14:6, 7) were the subject of prophecy—the prophecy of Revelation 10:5–11:1, which they believe identifies the present-day Advent movement as the "remnant" of Revelation 12:17.

Revelation 10 depicts an angel telling John to eat a little book that had to do with prophecy (see verse 11). The angel warned that the book would " 'make your stomach bitter, but it will be as sweet as honey in your mouth' " (Rev. 10:9). The Adventists who maintained their belief that God had been with them in their joyous though mistaken proclamation of Christ's imminent return in 1844 saw this prophecy as a prediction concerning their experience in the Advent movement. They saw in it the joy of expectation and awareness of God's blessing combined with the bitter disappointment they felt when Christ did not come on October 22, 1844. In addition, they came to believe that the measuring of "the temple of God, and the altar, and them that worship therein" predicted in Revelation 11:1 described the pre-Advent judgment that was to take place during the antitypical day of atonement.

If abandoning a mistaken belief is a fault, Seventh-day Adventists humbly acknowledge the charge—*but consider themselves in good company.* All through Christ's earthly ministry and right up to His ascension, His disciples mistakenly believed that He was going to set up an earthly kingdom in their day (see Acts 1:6). Yet Christ did not reject them on account of this misunderstanding. Why? Because when they realized their mistake, they abandoned their erroneous view and accepted truth. *This, we believe, is what the Sabbath-keeping Adventists did.* It is not the making of a mistake that disqualifies people from being God's remnant. It is the refusal to relinquish a misconception and the rejection of truth that explains that misconception that disqualifies a person, a church, a movement from being of God.

Seventh-day Adventists believe that their spiritual ancestors abandoned a misconception and embraced new truth when they gave up the belief that Christ would return to earth (spiritually or otherwise) on October 22, 1844 (see Matt. 24:36) and embraced the view that at the end of the 2,300 days/years Christ entered the Most Holy Place of heaven's sanctuary and that since that time He has been carrying forward the work of imparting (i.e., mediating) the benefits of the atonement gained at the Cross while carrying on the work of judgment in cleansing the heavenly sanctuary of the record of sin—as foretold in the prophecy of Daniel 8:14 and 7:9-13 (cp. Acts 2:19, 20).

Cleansing of the heavenly sanctuary

The book of Hebrews does not deal with the antitypical day of atonement in any great detail; nevertheless, it clearly teaches that there is a sanctuary in heaven where Christ ministers in behalf of sinners (see Heb. 8, 9). This biblical fact cannot be gainsaid, yet most Christians seem oblivious to it. Hebrews also teaches that the heavenly sanctuary and the people whose worship is directed there are as much in need of cleansing as were its earthly copy and the worshipers of Old Testament times (see Heb. 9:24, 25).

Knowledgeable Christians readily concede that the Passover met its antitype in the Crucifixion in the spring of the year (see 1 Cor. 5:9) and that the Feast of Weeks met its antitype on the Day of Pentecost, also in the spring (see Acts 1:3, 5; 2:1-4). Therefore, by parity of reasoning, the antitypical day of atonement must occur in the fall of the year, just as its type occurred in the fall. In other words, just as the earthly sanctuary was cleansed in the fall, so the cleansing of the heavenly sanctuary began in the fall. In the earthly sanctuary it was the Day of Atonement on which the sanctuary and the people were cleansed (see Lev. 16:2-34; 23:27-32). Seventh-day Adventists believe this work began on October 22, 1844, and will continue to go forward until the close of probation for the human race (see Rev. 22:11, 12).

What, then, is involved in this cleansing of the sanctuary? To answer this question, we must discuss the Hebrew word *nisdaq*.

The word *nisdaq,* rendered "declared right" in the clause "then is the holy place declared right" (Dan. 8:14, Young), occurs only in this verse in the Old Testament. It is derived from the root *tsadaq,* which basically means "righteousness." But in other forms this root has other meanings, such as "to be righteous" or "to be just" in the sense of justified (being made to appear righteous), and so on.

With this in mind, some scholars have translated the clause "then shall the sanctuary be made righteous" or "then shall the sanctuary be justified." But technically speaking, a *building*—a sanctuary—cannot be justified or be made righteous, because buildings don't sin. Only morally responsible beings can be justified or be made righteous, because only morally responsible beings are capable of sinning.

Recognizing this fact, recent translators have rendered *nisdaq* "be put in a right condition," "be restored to its rightful state," "be brought into its right condition," "be righted," etc. The question is: What did the term mean to the Jews living near Daniel's day?

The ancient Greek version of the Old Testament, the Septuagint, was translated by Hebrew scholars between 250 and 150 B.C. They rendered *nisdaq* "cleansed." Jerome (fl. A.D. 400), a Christian scholar, after discussing the meaning of this word with learned rabbis of his day, rendered the word "cleansed" in his Latin Vulgate translation of the Bible.

Why did these ancient scholars give *nisdaq* this meaning? Apparently for two interconnected reasons: 1) the word is undeniably used in connection with the sanctuary, and 2) *the sanctuary and the people* who worshiped there were ritually cleansed on the Day of Atonement (see Lev. 16:16-19).

The Day of Atonement and the pre-Advent judgment

The Day of Atonement was (and remains) a high day for every pious Jew. During its course the record of confessed sins, which figuratively had been accumulating in the sanctuary throughout the year through the various sin offerings, was symbolically removed, not only from the sanctuary, but also from the people. Thus cleansed of this record of sin, the people were made holy and the sanctuary was "restored to its rightful state."

The Day of Atonement, or Yom Kippur, was and is the most solemn occasion in the Jewish religious calendar. In his book *1844 Made Simple,* Clifford Goldstein, a Jew who is now a Seventh-day Adventist Christian, states that he has a Day of Atonement prayer book "filled with prayers devout Jews pray." Some of these prayers include such expressions as "justify us in the judgment," "silence the accuser [Satan]," "blot out the transgressions of the people that have been saved," and "He, the Ancient of Days, sits as Judge."[12]

According to Rabbi Yechiel Eckstein, Yom Kippur is the "final opportunity to come before God to plead for merciful *judgment*."[13] And the *Jewish Encyclopedia* quotes a liturgical piece as follows:

> "God, seated on His throne to judge the world, at the same time Judge, Pleader, Expert, and Witness, openeth the Book of Records; it is read, every man's signature being found therein. The great trumpet sounded; a still, small voice is heard; angels shudder, saying, this is *the day of judgment:* for His very ministers are not pure before God. As a shepherd mustereth his flock, causing them to pass under his rod, so doth God cause every living soul to pass before Him to fix the limit of every creature's life and to foreordain its destiny. On New Year's Day the decree is written; on the Day of Atonement it is sealed who shall live and who are to die, etc."[14]

Clearly, in the minds of pious Jews even in our day, the Day of Atonement is closely associated with *cleansing and judgment*. This association is not new. The fact that in ancient times anyone who on that day failed to engage in self-examination and to plead for cleansing from sin was to be "cut off" (Lev. 23:29) implies that it was more than simply a day for cleansing the sanctuary. It was a day of judgment; a day that separated the penitent from the impenitent.

The Cleansing of the Sanctuary and of the Remnant

In chapter 5 it was pointed out that the papal horn cast to the ground the truth concerning Christ's high priestly mediation in the heavenly sanctuary by substituting the oft-repeated sacrifice of the Mass in place of His "once for all" sacrifice on Calvary. During the 1,260 years of papal dominance, Christ's *tamid,* or continual mediation of the benefits of the atonement gained at the Cross, was in effect "taken from him" and "trampled under foot" by the "little horn" (see Dan. 8:9-12). This was done when the Roman hierarchy substituted the sacrifice of the Mass, a false sacerdotal system, and a false method of salvation—salvation by works—in place of Christ's once-for-all sacrifice on Calvary and His mediation on behalf of sinners. By so doing, the little horn figuratively defiled the heavenly sanctuary.

This explains why, from the earthly standpoint, judgment is executed against the little horn, while from the heavenly point of view, the sanctuary is cleansed from the record of the confessed sins of those who accept the benefits of Christ's atonement. At the end of this process, as the angel explained to Daniel, judgment will be given " 'in favor of the saints of the Most High' " (Dan. 7:22, NKJV). God's people are declared righteous, and subsequently, judgment is executed against the little horn.

Some critics point out that God is omniscient and has no need to review books of record in a pre-Advent judgment in order to determine who will be saved and who will be lost. That's true; "the Lord knoweth them that are his" (2 Tim. 2:19). But these critics overlook the fact that, while God knows all things, angels do not. This is the reason for the pre-Advent judgment. It is held so that *unfallen, but finite beings (angels, for instance) might be satisfied that sinners admitted to heaven are fit for the celestial abode!*

This explains why angels are present in the judgment scene of Daniel 7:9, 10. They are the witnesses as well as the jury in this great assize (see Eccl. 5:6; Matt. 18:10). It is they who testify concerning the accuracy of what is written in the books (see Dan. 7:10, Rev. 20:12). They have witnessed the great controversy between good and evil from its very inception. So, when heaven's court has examined what is written in the books concerning sinful human beings, they, together with the Ancient of Days, render a verdict in each case.

John the revelator speaks of this "hour of God's judgment" being proclaimed "while the everlasting gospel" is being preached to the inhabitants of earth (Rev. 14:6, 7). Obviously, this proclamation must precede the decree, " 'He who is unjust, let him be unjust still; he who is filthy, let him be filthy still; he who is righteous, let him be righteous still; he who is holy, let him be holy still. And behold, I am coming quickly, and My reward is with Me' " (Rev. 22:11, 12, NKJV). What could be clearer than that the judgment referred to here is a different judgment than that which takes place at the end of the millennium, as Arno Gaebelein declared?* That this judgment—or separation between the saved and the lost—takes place *before* the Second Advent is confirmed elsewhere in Scripture (see Matt. 22:2-14; Heb. 9:27, 28).

The point of it all

Seventh-day Adventists believe that John the revelator was personifying the Advent movement when he was told to take the little book in the angel's hand and eat it—in other words, to digest it and absorb its contents. That little book had to do with prophecy—the prophecy of Daniel 8:14, we believe. The Millerites, by diligent study of Daniel's prophecies, came to the mistaken conclusion that Christ was coming in 1843 or 1844. Just as the little book was sweet in the Revelator's mouth but bitter in his stomach, so this hope in Christ's imminent return was to the Millerites "sweet as honey," but it turned to "bitter" disappointment.

But this was not the end of the story. The angel instructed John, representing those who went through the disappointment of 1844, to "prophesy again" (verse 11). They had made a mistake, but God did not reject them on this account. Why? Because, when they realized their

---

* See page 39 above.

mistake, they abandoned it and accepted "present truth" as the Holy Spirit unfolded it to them.

So, their sweet-then-bitter experience and the command to "prophesy again," are, we believe, evidences that God has put Seventh-day Adventists in the world with a message for "many peoples, nations, tongues, and kings" (Rev. 10:11, NKJV). And this in spite of "mockers," who Scripture predicts were to arise "at [the] close of the [2,300] days," deriding the message of the pre-Advent judgment and the nearness of the Second Advent (2 Pet. 3:3, Darby; cp. Dan. 8:14; 12:13, Darby).

Seventh-day Adventists believe God has entrusted them with a worldwide mission—the proclamation that "the hour of . . . [God's pre-Advent] judgment has come" while also preaching "the everlasting gospel" to the inhabitants of earth (Rev. 14:6, 7, NKJV). And God has blessed! The major fragments of the Millerite movement have dwindled to virtually nothing. But the insignificant, despised minority who abandoned a misconception and accepted the good news concerning Christ's continual mediation in the heavenly sanctuary, the cleansing of that sanctuary, and the pre-Advent judgment has become a mighty movement with adherents numbering more than 11 million worldwide and still growing rapidly.

Perfect we are not. Nor do we claim that there is no salvation outside the Seventh-day Adventist Church; Christ has sheep in other folds. But we believe we are the people Bible prophecy predicted would rise in "the time of the end" proclaiming the everlasting gospel in the context of the pre-Advent judgment—*and calling God's people to "come out" of spiritual "Babylon," where human mediators try to replace the "one Mediator between God and men, himself man, Christ Jesus"* (1 Timothy 2:5, Confraternity).

The Seventh-day Adventist movement arose at the right time, "the time of the end"—immediately after October 22, 1844, to be precise—in fulfillment of the 2,300 days/years prophecy of Daniel 8:14. But this isn't all. The Great Disappointment that followed that date, rather than being evidence that God rejected the Sabbath-keeping Adventists, has proven to be their divine credential for proclaiming the gospel message in the context of the great antitypical day of atonement.

Thus, the preaching of "the everlasting gospel," in combination with the announcement that "the hour of . . . [God's] judgment has come"— *a judgment in which Christ, "the Son of man," appears before the Father, "the Ancient of Days," on our behalf as our faithful "Advocate,"* is a thrilling message of encouragement to every Christian who looks forward to "that blessed hope, and the glorious appearing of the great God and our Saviour Jesus Christ" (Titus 2:13). This is a distinctive message taught by no other church, and the reader is cordially invited to join Seventh-day Adventists in its worldwide proclamation.

"Even so, come, Lord Jesus."

1. *Prophetic Faith,* 4:208; see also 518. Emphasis in the original.

2. William Miller, *Wm. Miller's Apology and Defence* (Boston: J.V. Himes, 1845), 12.

3. William Miller, "Synopsis of Miller's Views," *Signs of the Times,* 4:47, Jan. 25, 1843.

4. "William Miller," *Seventh-day Adventist Encyclopedia,* Don F. Neufeld, ed. (Washington, D.C.: Review and Herald Publishing Association, 1976), 891.

5. [John Nelson Darby], *The 'Holy Scriptures' a New Translation From the Original Languages* (Hampton Wick, Kingston-on-Thames: Stow Hill Bible and Tract Depot, 1961).

6. Helen Spurrell, *A Translation of the Old Testament Scriptures From the Original Hebrew* (London: James Nisbet & Co., 1985). Emphasis supplied.

7. "Clovis I," *Encyclopedia Americana—International Edition* (Danbury, Connecticut: Grolier Incorporated, 1998), 7:121.

8. Lagard, *op. cit.,* vi.

9. "Samuel S. Snow," *SDA Enc.,* 1357.

10. *Prophetic Faith,* 4:879, 881.

11. Donald Grey Barnhouse, *Eternity,* Sept. 1956, 44.

12. Clifford Goldstein, *1844 Made Simple* (Nampa, Idaho: Pacific Press Publishing Association, 1988), 40.

13. Yechiel Eckstein, *Jews and Judaism* (Waco, Texas: Word Books, 1984), 125; quoted in Goldstein, *1844 Made Simple,* 40. Emphasis supplied.

14. "Atonement, Day of," *The Jewish Encyclopedia,* Isidore Singer, ed. (New York: Funk and Wagnalls Company, 1902), 2:286. Emphasis supplied.

Appendix

This appendix contains chapters 7–9 of the book of Daniel quoted in their entirety. Chapter 7 has been quoted from the New American Bible so the reader can see that, even in this Roman Catholic translation, it is apparent that the little horn—which arose among the horns that symbolized the tribes that replaced the Roman Empire—represents Antichrist.

Chapters 8 and 9 are quoted from Young's Literal Translation of the Holy Bible, one of the most literal translations available today. Readers may find this helpful in understanding the linked prophecies these two chapters contain—prophecies that reach to our own day.

Daniel 7

[1] In the first year of King Belshazzar of Babylon, Daniel had a dream as he lay in bed, and was terrified by the visions of his mind. Then he wrote down the dream; the account began: [2] In the vision I saw during the night, suddenly the four winds of heaven stirred up the great sea, [3] from which emerged four immense beasts, each different from the others. [4] The

first was like a lion, but with eagle's wings. While I watched, the wings were plucked; it was raised from the ground to stand on two feet like a man, and given a human mind. [5] The second was like a bear; it was raised up on one side, and among the teeth in its mouth were three tusks. It was given the order, "Up, devour much flesh." [6] After this I looked and saw another beast, like a leopard; on its back were four wings like those of a bird, and it had four heads. To this beast dominion was given. [7] After this, in the visions of the night I saw the fourth beast, different from all the others, terrifying, horrible, and of extraordinary strength; it had great iron teeth with which it devoured and crushed, and what was left it trampled with its feet. [8] I was considering the ten horns it had, when suddenly another, a little horn, sprang out of their midst, and three of the previous horns were torn away to make room for it. This horn had eyes like a man, and a mouth that spoke arrogantly.

[9] As I watched,
  Thrones were set up
and the Ancient One took his throne.
  His clothing was snow bright,
and the hair on his head as white as wool;
His throne was flames of fire,
with wheels of burning fire.
[10] A surging stream of fire
flowed out from where he sat;
  Thousands upon thousands were ministering
to him,
  and myriads upon myriads attended him.
The court was convened, and the books were opened. [11] I watched, then, from the first of the arrogant words which the horn spoke, until the beast was slain and its body thrown into the fire to be burnt up. [12] The other beasts, which also lost

their dominion, were granted a prolongation of life for a time and a season. [13] As the visions during the night continued, I saw

> One like a son of man coming,
> on the clouds of heaven;
> When he reached the Ancient One
> and was presented before him,
> [14] He received dominion, glory, and kingship;
> nations and peoples of every language serve
>   him.
> His dominion is an everlasting dominion
> that shall not be taken away,
> his kingship shall not be destroyed.

[15] I, Daniel, found my spirit anguished within its sheath of flesh, and I was terrified by the visions of my mind. [16] I approached one of those present and asked him what all this meant in truth; in answer, he made known to me the meaning of the things: [17] "These four great beasts stand for four kingdoms which shall arise on the earth. [18] But the holy ones of the Most High shall receive the kingship, to possess it forever and ever."

[19] But I wished to make certain about the fourth beast, so very terrible and different from the others, devouring and crushing with its iron teeth and bronze claws, and trampling with its feet what was left; [20] about the ten horns on its head, and the other one that sprang up, before which three horns fell; about the horn with the eyes and the mouth that spoke arrogantly, which appeared greater than its fellows. [21] For, as I watched, that horn made war against the holy ones and was victorious [22] until the Ancient One arrived; judgment was pronounced in favor of the holy ones of the Most High, and the time came when the holy ones possessed the kingdom. [23] He answered me thus:

"The fourth beast shall be a fourth kingdom on earth,
different from all the others;
It shall devour the whole earth,
beat it down, and crush it.
[24] The ten horns shall be ten kings
rising out of that kingdom;
another shall rise up after them,
Different from those before him,
Who shall lay low three kings.
[25] He shall speak against the Most High
and oppress the holy ones of the Most High,
thinking to change the feast days and the law.
They shall be handed over to him
for a year, two years, and a half-year.
[26] But when the court is convened,
and his power is taken away
by final and absolute destruction,
[27] Then the kingship and dominion and majesty
of all the kingdoms under the heavens
shall be given to the holy people of the Most High,
whose kingdom shall be everlasting:
All dominions shall serve and obey him."
[28] The report concluded: I, Daniel, was greatly terrified by my thoughts, and my face blanched, but I kept the matter to myself.

—*The Catholic Study Bible: New American Study Bible,* Donald Senior, gen. ed. (New York: Oxford University Press). Nihil Obstat, Rev. John G. Lodge, Rev. Robert L. Schoenstene; Imprimatur, Rev. P. Roache, November 27, 1989.

Appendix

Daniel 8:1–10:1

VIII ¹ "IN the third year of the reign of Belshazzar the king, a vision hath appeared unto me—I Daniel—after that which had appeared unto me at the beginning. ² And I see in a vision, and it cometh to pass, in my seeing, and I *am* in Shushan the palace that *is* in Elam the province, and I see in a vision, and I have been by the stream Ulai. ³ And I lift up mine eyes, and look, and lo, a certain ram is standing before the stream, and it hath two horns, and the two horns *are* high; and the one *is* higher than the other, and the high one is coming up last. ⁴ I have seen the ram pushing westward, and northward, and southward, and no living creatures do stand before it, and there is none delivering out of its hand, and it hath done according to its pleasure, and hath exerted itself.

⁵ "And I have been considering, and lo, a young he-goat hath come from the west, over the face of the whole earth, whom none is touching in the earth; as to the young he-goat, a conspicuous horn *is* between its eyes. ⁶ And it cometh unto the ram possessing the two horns, that I had seen standing before the stream, and runneth unto it in the fury of its power. ⁷ And I have seen it coming near the ram, and it becometh embittered at it, and smiteth the ram, and breaketh its two horns, and there hath been no power in the ram to stand before it, and it casteth it to the earth, and trampleth it down, and there hath been no deliverer to the ram out of its power.

⁸ "And the young he-goat hath exerted itself very much, and when it is strong, broken hath been the great horn; and come up doth a vision of four in its place, at the four winds of the heavens. ⁹ And from the one of them come forth hath a little horn, and it exerteth itself greatly toward the south, and toward the east, and toward the beauteous *land;* ¹⁰ yea, it exerteth unto the host of the heavens, and causeth to fall to the earth of the

host, and of the stars, and trampleth them down. [11] And unto the prince of the host it exerteth itself, and by it taken away hath been the continual *sacrifice,* and thrown down the base of his sanctuary. [12] And the host is given up, with the continual *sacrifice,* through transgression, and it throweth down truth to the earth, and it hath worked, and prospered.

[13] "And I hear a certain holy one speaking, and a certain holy one saith to the wonderful numberer who is speaking: Till when *is* the vision of the continual *sacrifice,* and of the transgression, an astonishment, to make both sanctuary and host a treading down? [14] And he saith unto me, Till evening-morning two thousand and three hundred, then is the holy place declared right.

[15] "And it cometh to pass in my seeing—I, Daniel—the vision, that I require understanding, and lo, standing over-against me *is* as the appearance of a mighty one. [16] And I hear a voice of man between *the banks of* Ulai, and he calleth and saith: Gabriel, cause this *one* to understand the appearance. [17] And he cometh in near my station, and at his coming in I have been afraid, and I fall on my face, and he saith unto me: Understand, son of man, for at the time of the end *is* the vision. [18] And in his speaking with me, I have been in a trance on my face, on the earth; and he cometh against me, and causeth me to stand on my station, [19] and saith: Lo, I—I am causing thee to know that which is in the latter end of the indignation; for, at the appointed time *is* the end.

[20] "The ram that thou hast seen possessing two horns, *are* the kings of Media and Persia. [21] And the young he-goat, the hairy one, *is* the king of Javan [Greece]; and the great horn that *is* between its eyes is the first king; [22] and that being broken, stand up do four in its place, four kingdoms from the nation do stand up, and not in its power.

²³ "And in the latter end of their kingdom, about the perfecting of the transgressors, stand up doth a king, fierce of face, and understanding hidden things; ²⁴ and his power hath been mighty, and not by his own power; and wonderful things he destroyeth, and he hath prospered, and wrought, and destroyed mighty ones, and the people of the Holy Ones.

²⁵ "And by his understanding he hath also caused deceit to prosper in his hand, and in his heart he exerteth himself, and by ease he destroyeth many; and against the prince of princes he standeth—and without hand he is broken. ²⁶ And the appearance of the evening and of the morning, that is told, is true; and thou, hide thou the vision, for *it is* after many days."

²⁷ And I, Daniel, have been, yea, I became sick *for* days, and I rise, and do the king's work, and *am* astonished at the appearance, and there is none understanding.

IX. ¹ IN the first year of Darius, son of Ahasuerus, of the seed of the Medes, who hath been made king over the kingdom of the Chaldeans, ² in the first year of his reign, I, Daniel, have understood by books the number of the years, (in that a word of Jehovah hath been unto Jeremiah the prophet,) concerning the fulfilling of the wastes of Jerusalem—seventy years; ³ and I set my face unto the Lord God, to seek *by* prayer and supplications, with fasting, and sackcloth, and ashes.

⁴ And I pray to Jehovah my God, and confess, and say: "I beseech Thee, O Lord God, the great and the fearful, keeping the covenant and the kindness to those loving Him, and to those keeping His commands; ⁵ we have sinned, and done perversely, and done wickedly, and rebelled, to turn aside from Thy commands, and from Thy judgments: and we have not hearkened unto Thy servants, the prophets, who have spoken in Thy name unto our kings, our heads, and our fathers, and to all the people of the land.

[7] "To Thee, O Lord *is* the righteousness, and to us the shame of face, as *at* this day, to the men of Judah, and to the inhabitants of Jerusalem, and to all Israel, who are near, and who are far off, in all the lands whither Thou has driven them, in their trespass that they have trespassed against Thee.

[8] "O Lord, to us *is* the shame of face, to our kings, to our heads, and to our fathers, in that we have sinned against Thee.

[9] "To the Lord our God *are* the mercies and the forgivenesses, for we have rebelled against Him, [10] and have not hearkened to the voice of Jehovah our God, to walk in His laws, that He hath set before us by the hand of His servants the prophets; [11] and all Israel have transgressed Thy law, to turn aside so as not to hearken to Thy voice; and poured on us is the execration, and the oath, that is written in the law of Moses, servant of God, because we have sinned against Him.

[12] "And He confirmeth His words that He hath spoken against us, and against our judges who have judged us, to bring in upon us great evil, in that it hath not been done under the whole heavens as it hath been done in Jerusalem, [13] as it is written in the law of Moses, all this evil hath come upon us, and we have not appeased the face of Jehovah our God to turn back from our iniquities, and to act wisely in Thy truth, [14] And Jehovah doth watch for the evil, and bringeth it upon us, for righteous *is* Jehovah our God concerning all His works that He hath done, and we have not hearkened to His voice. [15] And now, O Lord our God, who hast brought forth Thy people from the land of Egypt by a strong hand, and dost make for Thee a name as at this day, we have sinned, we have done wickedly.

[16] "O Lord, according to all Thy righteous acts, let turn back, I pray Thee, Thine anger and Thy fury from Thy city Jerusalem, Thy holy mount, for by our sins, and by the iniq-

uities of our fathers, Jerusalem and Thy people *are* for a re-
proach to all our neighbours; [17] and now, hearken, O our God,
unto the prayer of Thy servant, and unto his supplications,
and cause Thy face to shine on Thy sanctuary that *is* desolate,
for the Lord's sake.

[18] "Incline, O my God, Thine ear, and hear, open Thine
eyes and see our desolations, and the city on which Thy name is
called; for not for our righteous acts are we causing our supplications to fall before Thee, but for Thy mercies that *are* many. [19]
O Lord, hear, O Lord, forgive; O Lord, attend and do; do not
delay, for Thine own sake, O my God, for Thy name is called
on Thy city, and on Thy people."

[20] And while I am speaking, and praying, and confessing
my sin, and the sin of my people Israel, and causing my suppli-
cation to fall before Jehovah my God, for the holy mount of my
God, [21] yea, while I am speaking in prayer, then that one Gabriel,
whom I had seen in vision at the commencement, being caused
to fly swiftly, is coming unto me at the time of the evening
present.

[22] And he giveth understanding, and speaketh with me,
and saith, "O Daniel, now I have come forth to cause thee to
consider understanding wisely; [23] at the commencement of
thy supplications hath the word come forth, and I have come
to declare *it,* for thou *art* greatly desired, and understand
thou concerning the matter, and consider concerning the
appearance.

[24] "Seventy weeks are determined for thy people, and for
thy holy city, to shut up the transgression, and to seal up
sins, and to cover iniquity, and to bring in righteousness age-
during, and to seal up vision and prophet, and to anoint the
holy of holies. [25] And thou dost know, and doest consider
wisely, from the going forth of the word to restore and to
build Jerusalem till Messiah the Leader *is* seven weeks, and

sixty and two weeks: the broad place hath been built again, and the rampart, even in the distress of the times. [26] And after the sixty and two weeks, cut off is Messiah, and the city and the holy place are not his, the Leader who hath come doth destroy the people; and its end *is* with a flood, and till the end *is* war, determined *are* desolations. And he hath strengthened a covenant with many—one week, and *in* the midst of the week he causeth sacrifice and present to cease, and by the wing of abominations he is making desolate, even till the consummation, and that which is determined is poured on the desolate one."

X. [1] IN the third year of Cyrus king of Persia, a thing is revealed to Daniel, whose name is called Belteshazzar, and the thing is true, and the warfare *is* great: and he hath understood the thing and hath understanding about the appearance."*

(All italics in the above are in the original.)

—Robert Young, *Young's Literal Translation of the Bible,* rev. ed. (Grand Rapids, Michigan: Baker Book House, 1956). All italics in the above are in the original.

---

*Note that three years after the vision of the seventy weeks was given Daniel said that he understood the "appearance" *(mareh),* the vision. In other words, he said he finally understood the significance of the 2,300 days/years vision. Here, again, we see a link between Daniel 8 and 9. (See chapter 6 above, particularly pages 64, 65.)

If you enjoyed this book,
you'll enjoy these as well:

Adventists & Armageddon
Donald E. Mansell investigates the metamorphosis in doctrinal interpretation that has taken place within Adventism regarding earth's final battle. He contrasts the historical views on this subject and provides a warning for Adventists to tread lightly when it comes to unfulfilled prophecy.

0-8163-1684-8. Paperback. US$10.99, Cdn$16.49. Study guide US$.99, Cdn$1.49.

The Shape of the Coming Crisis
Donald E. Mansell. This book shows a sequence of end-time events based on the writings of Ellen G. White. It's in-depth study of the Spirit of Prophecy shows that end-time events are already beginning to happen.

0-8163-1402-0. Paper. US$12.99, Cdn$18.99.

The Great Compromise
Clifford Goldstein. In his most provocative and poignant work, Clifford Goldstein reveals how evangelicals are compromising the foundational truth of justification by faith alone for political purposes, and exposes the documents they are using to "heal the deadly wound" with Rome.

0-8163-1821-2. Paperback. US$10.99, Cdn$16.49.

Order from your ABC by calling **1-800-765-6955**, or get online and shop our virtual store at **www.adventistbookcenter.com**.
- Read a chapter from your favorite book
- Order online
- Sign up for email notices on new products